PRAGMATIC ASPECTS OF HUMAN COMMUNICATION

THEORY AND DECISION LIBRARY

VOLUME 4

PRAGMATIC ASPECTS
OF HUMAN COMMUNICATION

Edited by

COLIN CHERRY

Imperial College of Science and Technology, London

D. REIDEL PUBLISHING COMPANY

DORDRECHT-HOLLAND/BOSTON-U.S.A.

Library of Congress Catalog Card Number 73–91427

Cloth edition: ISBN 90 277 0432 5
Paperback edition: ISBN 90 277 0520 8

Published by D. Reidel Publishing Company,
P.O. Box 17, Dordrecht, Holland

Sold and distributed in the U.S.A., Canada and Mexico
by D. Reidel Publishing Company, Inc.
306 Dartmouth Street, Boston,
Mass. 02116, U.S.A.

Printed in The Netherlands by D. Reidel, Dordrecht

CONTENTS

PREFACE

'Human Communication' is a field of interest of enormous breadth, being one which has concerned students of many different disciplines. It spans the imagined 'gap' between the 'arts' and the 'sciences', but it forms no unified academic subject. There is no commonly accepted terminology to cover all aspects.

The eight articles comprising this book have been chosen to illustrate something of the diversity yet, at the same time, to be comprehensible to readers from different academic disciplines. They cannot pretend to cover the whole field! Some attempt has been made to present them in an order which represents a continuity of theme, though this is merely an opinion.

Most publications of this type form the proceedings of some symposium, or conference. In this case, however, there has been no such unifying influence, no collaboration, no discussions. The authors have been drawn from a number of different countries.

The first article, by John Marshall and Roger Wales (Great Britain) concerns the *pragmatic* values of communication, starting by considering bird-song and passing to the infinitely more complex 'meaningful' values of human language and pictures. The 'pragmatic aspect' means the usefulness – what does language or bird song *do* for humans and birds? What adaptation or survival values does it have? These questions are then considered in relation to brain specialisation for representation of experience and cognition.

The second article, by Isaak Revzin of the U.S.S.R. enquires into the old question of the origins of human language. Some there may be who argue that no purpose is served by such enquiry because we cannot make experimental checks of such hypotheses. But the same comment was made by Henry Ford about history – that "History is bunk"; yet this belief does not justify the immediate dismissal of all historians.

The third article, by Dennis Dicks, a Canadian psychologist, describes procedures for making laboratory experiments upon human conversation. To me it is remarkable that conversation, which is probably the commonest phenomenon in nature within human experience, should be so difficult to study under laboratory conditions. Most experiments upon speech have used the utterances of single isolated persons, whilst the truly natural unit, the two-person conversation has been sadly neglected.

The fourth article, contributed by Aaron Cicourel of the U.S.A. also describes experiments into real-life communication, but this time into the highly ritualised forms we call 'interviewing' and 'fixed-choice questionnaires', techniques so commonly used in social science. In this article, it is medical interviews and questionnaires that are examined, showing the many sources of misunderstanding and error that may occur, with many illustrative examples.

Human language is infinite in its values, purposes and styles. The phenomenal thing about it is that it *works*. With it we may inform, insult, threaten, cajole, reconcile, conceal, move, frighten, – talk to ourselves, think and deceive ourselves. In the fifth article, by Solomon Marcus of Romania, the polar extremes of scientific language and poetic language are compared and contrasted – both belonging (in his words) "to the family of languages of discovery". It is the fact that art and science are both concerned with discovery, yet appear to be so diverse in method, that makes this comparison the more interesting.

The sixth article, by Merrill Garrett of the U.S.A., describes an experimental enquiry into the old question: "What happens when we 'understand sentences'?" Language is 'meaningful'; it works. Yet we never fully understand everything implied by a stream of speech; it can always be enlarged upon, expanded. We accept such meaning from it as suits our particular purpose of the moment. The experiments described enquire into the mental processes that may occur during perception of spoken sentences, rendering them meaningful.

Kenneth Forster, of Australia, contributes the seventh article, which is concerned with the *production* of sentences. As with conversation studies in the laboratory, the controlled production of spontaneous speech for experimental purposes is equally difficult. And it is the speech itself that may be observed directly, not the thoughts or intentions of the speaker which have led to its production. Some indirect approaches to the problem are described, which cast light on to the ways in which thought becomes unfolded and revealed in syntactic structures.

The eight, and final, article is by Jacob Marschak, of U.S.A., an economist and statistician; it is entitled 'Information, Decision, and the Scientist'. This article differs somewhat from the others, inasmuch as it is concerned with extraction of information from scientific experiments. Strictly speaking we do not 'communicate' with Mother Nature (for we share no language with her) but, nevertheless, there is a great deal in common between the theory of communication and the theory of observation. We form and test hypotheses, gather evidence, infer and value in both cases (what else can we do?). The philosophical and mathematical arguments here may tell us little about the structure of language but they are more relevant to the question as to why language works.

These brief remarks are not intended as single paragraph summaries of these eight papers, nor do they necessarily express the opinions of their writers. They can do no more than vaguely illustrate the immense breadth of the field of 'human communication' and something of the great diversity of studies it has produced. Perhaps the book can do no more than indicate to students of one discipline something of the interests, of the problems, and of the methods of their fellows in other disciplines. If it does this, it will have succeeded, for nothing is more certain than that researches in any one branch of 'human communication' urgently require sympathy with the problems and purposes of other branches.

JOHN C. MARSHALL AND ROGER J. WALES

PRAGMATICS AS BIOLOGY OR CULTURE

ABSTRACT. Charles Morris's tripartite definition of pragmatics (origin, uses and effects of signs) [28] is considered in the context of the biological prerequisites of language, and the organization of language-learning. The structure of animal and human communication systems is discussed in relation to brain specialization for the representation of different aspects of experience and cognition

I. CONCERNING ORIGINS

The glossary to Charles Morris's *Signs, Language and Behaviour* [28] gives the following well-known definition of pragmatics: "That branch of semiotic which studies the origin, the uses, and the effects of signs. It is distinguished from semantics and syntactics." We might reasonably construe questions of origin (both phylogenetic and ontogenetic) as falling within the domain of evolutionary biology, and questions of use and effect as falling within the domain of social psychology. There must, however, be interactions between these two domains. Given the paradigm of Neo-Darwinian theory, the notions of use and effect (i.e. survival and adaption value) are crucial to an understanding of how *ordered* change can result from (pragmatically) *random* mutation. Within this framework there would appear to be few (if any) *conceptual* problems associated with current explanations of the simplest forms of sign-stimulus behaviour in lower animals. It is not difficult to imagine that a genetic mutation could result in a worm or ant excreting a chemical trail when replete with food; granted certain constraints on the production-perception mechanisms, it is easy to conceive that such an ant would find these trails attractive. Given that the mutation arises in more than one member of the species, one can see how the system might confer a selective advantage upon the organisms possessing it. (For examples of pheromone communication, and discussion of the *scientific* problems involved in understanding them, see [3]. The details of such systems – e.g. that successful food-foraging trails should lose their potency very quickly [3], but 'alarm'-trails retain their aversive properties over a period of months [35] – are comprehen-

C. Cherry (ed.), Pragmatic Aspects of Human Communication, 1–13. *All Rights Reserved*
Copyright © 1974 *by D. Reidel Publishing Company, Dordrecht-Holland*

sible, even if not fully understood, within the Neo-Darwinian paradigm. It can readily be seen that the main reason for this is that minimal (or zero) *learning* of the formal properties of the communication-system and of the 'meaning' of its messages is required. Now we move to an example where the structure of *experience* is crucial to the acquisition of the system.

'Full-song' is acquired by a white-crowned sparrow if and only if the juvenile bird is exposed to adult song during a fairly well defined 'sensitive period'; in the absence of such experience, the socially isolated (but otherwise intact) bird will produce, when mature, simple, phrased song, lacking the full dialect complexities of its normally reared conspecifics. A juvenile exposed to *any* white-crowned sparrow dialect learns that dialect; but exposure to the song of *another species* has little or no effect – the bird sings simple song when mature, just as if it had been totally isolated from experience of song. Once a system of this nature is in operation one can see how it is maintained, and one can speculate intelligibly (but at the moment not conclusively) about the functions it serves. Reviewing the literature from field experiments, Marler [23] notes that "it begins to look as though one result of song learning is an increase in the likelihood that male and female sparrows will settle in the area where they were born. This might lead to a minor degree of inbreeding in local populations, perhaps permitting the evolution of physiological adaptations to local conditions....'

However, whilst the maintenance of such systems is not conceptually puzzling, the *initial* origin is. How did the very first bird which produced full-song originate if experience of full-song is a prerequisite for its acquisition? Some kind of 'directed boot-strapping' is required. We can think of this process [23, 30] as involving a partial relaxation of constraints over motor output such that a degree of 'improvisation' [24] around the 'genetically-determined' theme becomes possible. For the system to stabilize, the theme must define the range of possible variations compatiable with it. Furthermore, as Nottebohm remarks, "... the genome must also specify that the vocal output must be altered until the auditory feedback it generates conforms to a particular pattern" [30]. Finally, there must be co-ordinated change between, at least, the form of relaxation of a fixed motor pattern, the structure of the acoustic specification, and the nature of the 'error-signals' which ensure eventual convergence upon a theme-compatible variation.

The Marler-Nottebohn approach thus seems to define a number of potentially answerable questions. Some of these are essentially syntactic, e.g. what is the formal structure of the relationship between full-song and sub-song for a particular species? Others concern the interpretation of genetic information, e.g. what, in terms of a putative mechanism, does 'a loosening of genetic control over motor development' mean? [30]. Yet others concern what one might call biological 'systems theory', namely the mechanisms of 'co-ordinated change' between the different aspects of the system.

It is crucial to the explanatory success of such a theory that the relationship between sub-song and full-song be fairly close. Unless subsong severely constrains the range of 'frills' which are compatible with it (i.e. *possible* elaborations), it is difficult to see how the system could evolve in an orderly fashion. It is similarly crucial that the endpoint (full-song under the combined control of a genetically determined base pattern, an auditory (or articulatory?) template, and a convergence mechanism) and all postulated evolutionary stages leading to the endpoint, should have specifiable adaptive function, cashable in terms of breeding success.

These two points, one syntactic and the other pragmatic, are presumably relevent to discussion of the supposed evolution of human language. But now the problems magnify out of all proportion. It could, for example, be argued that the only aspect of human language that is 'built in', *in the same sense that sub-song is built in*, is babbling. The sense in which Chomsky argues for "the conception of universal grammar as an innate schematism ..." [6] is a quite different interpretation of the notion of innateness; namely that "... we must attribute to the organism, as an innate property, a structure rich enough to account for the fact that the postulated grammar is acquired *on the basis of the given conditions of access to data*" [7], (our italics). The data for the acquisition of English are the utterances of people speaking English, and the relationship of English to babbling is, to put it mildly, rather more distant than the relationship between full- and sub-song. The problem of understanding how relevent environments could have come into existence is thus correspondingly greater; one can see, all too easily, why the Statutes of the Paris Société de Linguistique (1866) contain the famous prohibition "La Société n'admet aucune communication concernant... l'origine du langage".

Some scholars, on the assumption that the original proto-language of *homo sapiens* was not vocal, have recently been heartened by the remarkable achievements of the Gardners' [12] and Premack's [33] chimpanzees. It may be instructive, however, to think of the complexity of the human culture which is a prerequisite for the appearance of the abilities shown by Washoe and Sarah – note that the title of Premack's paper is 'Some General Characteristics of a Method for Teaching Language to Organisms which do not Ordinarily Acquire it' [33]. Could a Skinnerian methodology have been formulated and applied by creatures not in possession of a language and a verbally articulated 'science of behaviour'? As a counter to this line of attack, Hewes argues: "For a language to appear within three or four years in a young chimpanzee may indeed require these advanced specialized conditions. It is reasonable, however, to suppose that the building of a simple gestural language in the proto-hominids took place not within three or four years, but over perhaps some *millions* of years, under suitable environmental conditions" [18].

This type of argument is, of course, one of the most fascinating fallacies in much Neo-Darwinian debate: If one cannot conceive of a *mechanism* whereby a particular ability came into existence, one claims that it took a long time to evolve. (It is interesting that this is the same fallacy, only standing on its head, as the once popular 'deduction': children acquire language quickly; therefore language is innate.)

It seems unlikely that a direct attack on the problem of the 'evolution' of human language will be successful; the *primary* data are simply not available. Perhaps instead one might develop an approach to an adequate theory via what might be called 'conceptual neurology'. What, then, can be said about the prerequisites of language from such a viewpoint?

II. PRAGMATICS AND THE BRAIN

In the 18th and 19th Centuries arguments of the following nature were frequently advanced: "If man had the drives of the animals, he could not have what we now call reason in him; for such drives would pull his forces darkly toward a single point, in such a way that he would have no free sphere of awareness. If man had the senses of the animals, he would have no reason; for the keen alertness of his senses and the mass of perceptions flooding him would smother all cool reflection" [17]. Steinthal [37] preserves the metaphor; the senses of animals "are wide gates through which external nature rushes to the assault with such impetus as to overwhelm the mind and deprive it of all independence and freedom of movement."

These notions have re-emerged in more recent speculation. For example, the inhibition of 'drives' (or emotive representations of experience) is crucial to Geschwind's interpretation [13, 14] of the neurological prerequisites of 'objective naming'. Thus Geschwind claims that the striking development in man of cortico-cortical connections between brain areas serving different modalities (e.g. visual-auditory) provides a mechanism for simple non-emotive naming; he contrasts this state of affairs with the neurological organization of lower primates in which it is claimed that cross-modal association must take place via the 'limbic system', a collection of sub-cortical structures subserving basic emotional responses (anger, fear) and appetites (hunger, thirst, sexual desire etc.). In essence, this view would argue that the domain of the coding in which interactions between modalities take place is emotive in lower animals but semantic in man. Geschwind's ideas have not, however, found favour among all neuropsychologists, and Pribram [34], for example, proposes a radically different view of the structure and phylogeny of brain-organization. (Herder had been well aware of the problems involved in arguing from structure to function, cf. his remark "should physiology ever progress to the point where it can demonstrate psychology – which I greatly doubt ..." [17].)

Likewise, one can see a direct link between Herder's notion of 'vivid perceptions smothering cool reflection' and current theorizing concerning the significance of hemispheric specialization in man. Thus it is known that, in some sense, the left hemisphere is specialized for dealing with linguistic (propositional) structure, that is, speech and writing; the right hemisphere for dealing with visuo-spatial (non-propositional) and musical structures. (Bogen [2] discusses a set of alternative hypotheses which have been proposed for the differences underlying the respective performances of the hemispheres.)

Furthermore, it would appear that the development of hemispheric specialization may lead to different kinds of *interpretation* of emotional states. (If this is correct, implications would seem to follow for the controversy concerning the functional independence of cortical and sub-cortical systems.) The Italian literature [38, 11] suggests that injury to the two hemispheres results in different emotional reactions; left-hemisphere injury (or inactivation by pharmacological means) is associated with 'depressive-catastrophic' reactions, whilst right-hemisphere injury or inactivation produces 'euphoric-maniacal' reactions with stated indifference to, or even denial of, the resulting functional disorder. One might argue, then, that the right-hemisphere's reaction to its injured other half is 'normal' (that is, the affect is appropriate) but the 'intellectual' left-hemisphere gives a very different interpretation to the disability of the right-hemisphere. It is not without interest that results of the above type are apparently difficult to replicate among phlegmatic North Americans [27]. The way we are made, in interaction with our cultural experience, seems to truly affect the way we seen the world.

Returning to *formal* differences between the types of representation characteristic of the two hemispheres' information-processing capacities, Levy [21] has suggested that there may be a 'competitive antagonism' between mechanisms required for 'Gestalt apprehension' of visuo-spatial relationships and for the 'analytic' strategies needed for the perception and production of language. If this is so, it would help to explain the frequently reported correlation between failure of hemispheric specialization and developmental disorders of linguistic and visuo-spatial skills (see [26] for references and discussion).

If the distinction between visuo-spatial and linguistic representations is basic in terms of the topology of brain-organization, one might inquire whether the dichotomy is of similar importance functionally. That is, what is the *utility* to the organism of having these two modes of representation? What can be done with linguistic representations that cannot be achieved with pictorial representations (and *vice versa*)?

III. PRAGMATIC DIFFERENCES BETWEEN LINGUISTIC AND PICTORIAL EXPRESSIONS

The history of art shows that there is more than one way of representing (objective) depth, just as the psychology of perception shows that there is more than one environmental cue available to the organism from which it can infer depth. Thus one cannot assume that the pictorial expressions of a culture are in any straightforward way isomorphic with the perceptual capacities of its people. From the fact that Egyptian paintings do not follow our conventions for perspective one cannot infer a perceptual deficiency in the artists responsible for these objects. In our own culture, the fact that children at a certain age typically leave out the torso in their drawings of people should at least make one wary of any simple views about the relationship of percepts to their overt representations.

It would be similarly mistaken to argue that pictorial representations must of necessity be less 'abstract' than linguistic representations. The distinction between convention and (more or less veridical) depiction is crucial to the understanding of many art forms (and many pictorial devices in science and technology). Pictures of Tutankahmun with his head apparently within his own bow are not to be interpreted as examples of faulty (indeed suicidal) archery technique; rather the convention marks the importance of the figure depicted – religious laws forbade the depiction of the faces of gods with lines drawn across them. Individual pictorial expressions are no more restricted to straightforward depiction than spoken languages are restricted to, say, onomatapoeic signs. The two systems do not differ in having or not having formal constraints which determine what can be represented: each one has its own culturally-shared syntax. Rather, the two forms of expression seem to differ with respect to the availability of *general systems* of conventions for assigning interpretations to them which would be likely to be generally shared by others of that culture. In language, the conventions for calling attention to what is important, to what is new, to the intended order in which information is to be processed, for conveying information about the presuppositions and expectations of the speaker etc., etc., all fit together into a coherent pattern. These pragmatic patterns, indicated by word-order, syntactic-form, stress, choice of article, choice of marked or un-marked lexical item and many other devices, are studied in linguistics under the rubric 'functional sentence perspective' [10, 16, 20]. To under-stand a natural language is, in part, to be able to distinguish the *propositional* content of a sentence (or text) from its pragmatic implications. In the famous example 'The train was not late this morning' the force of the presupposition for appropriate use is particularly clear [42]. For further behavioural correlates of the propositional/pragmatic distinction, see Johnson-Laird [19] for the effect of word order, Wales [40] for the effect of which article is used, and Nash [29] for the significance of intonation as a cue to intended interpretation. To say this of natural language is not to deny that individual conventions are to be found in pictorial art (and technology) – size may denote not objective but rather conceptual size (importance); composition may act as a focussing device. Rather we are claiming that there appears to be no general set of interacting pictorial conventions which specify the pragmatic functions of an expression with the same degree of precision and clarity that attends, for example, the communicative consequences of optional transformations in linguistic structure.

Let us illustrate with a simple example the *systematic* nature of pragmatic relationships in natural language and how this contrasts with the structure of pictorial expression: Imagine the pictorial correlate of 'A square to the right of a triangle'; now consider 'A triangle to the left of a square'. The content stays constant, the topic changes as a function of phrase-order and lexical choice. Given a prior context in which we were already talking about squares and triangles, it is possible to use both definiteness and word-order to focus attention on the topic of discussion by saying 'The square to the right of the triangle'. Note also that one device, contrastive stress, can be used to emphasize any lexical item of a sentence, and that nouns may or may not.be modified by optional specifiers (e.g. adjectives) which further restrict the referential domain of the noun phrase. Gombrich [15] provides an excellent discussion of some of these differences between linguistic and pictorial expression: "... the sentence from the primer 'The cat sits on the mat' is certainly not abstract, but although the primer may show a picture of a cat sitting on a mat, a moment's reflection will show that the picture is not the equivalent of the statement. We cannot express whether we mean 'the' cat (an individual) or 'a' cat (a member of the class); moreover, although the sentence may be one possible description of the picture, there are an infinite number of other true descriptive statements you could make such as 'There is a cat seen from behind' or for that matter 'There is no elephant on the mat'."

As far as we can see, the only *generally* available visuo-spatial device for performing some of the above pragmatic functions is pointing (with the finger or chin according to the culture). The precision and range of this device clearly falls far short of what is available in language.

Yet it would clearly be false to suggest that in all respects and for all purposes linguistic expressions are superior to pictorial expressions. There are many situations in which, in the old cliché, one picture is worth a thousand words. Gombrich's most beautiful example is of a medieval 'tree of affinities' for representing genealogical relationships [15] Such trees *show* the structure of familial groupings with far greater lucidity than the equivalent linguistic expressions. Man's intellectual superiority may derive not so much from language-capacity *per se* but rather from having (at least) two distinct modes of representation, each appropriate to a different domain of problem-solving. Although in some ways separated into two hemispheres, the two representational modes presumably interact in the normal human brain – the outcomes of information processed in one mode can be passed to the other half brain for the elaboration of those aspects of the task to which it is more suited. In this way, the power of half a brain plus half a brain might be greater than one. But an interesting question then arises for students of localization of function: What is the language or notation in which a device specialized for operating in terms of visuo-spatial codes can transmit the results of its computations to a device specialized for operating in a linguistic code (and *vice versa*)? Current empirical studies [32, 8] are beginning to explore the psychological constraints on the two systems and the way in which they interact in judgment and memory tasks using latency measures. These measurements, though useful, do not seem sufficiently rich in terms of the information they yield to provide answers to many of the structural questions concerning the language of interaction between the codes.

Finally, let us place some of these issues in a developmental perspective. Most studies of language-acquisition have asked 'What can the child do with language itself', that is, which structures can he comprehend, manipulate and produce at different stages. An alternative tradition (that of Piaget and Vygotsky *par excellence*) has asked the inverse question 'What can language do for the child?', that is, what are the consequences with respect to the child's other behavioural capacities of his having access to a linguistic representation. (See Ryan [36] for an excellent discussion of communicative competence.) It is a commonplace among students of cognitive development to assign a crucial role to the acquisition of language. Thus Piaget, who does not accord a strictly central place to language in the development of operational (mathematical) thought, nevertheless concludes that "language is without doubt a necessary condition for the achievement of structures of a certain level (hypothetico-deductive and propositional)" [1]. Vygotsky [39], Luria [22], and Bruner [5] have all in different ways accorded to language a more central role in cognitive development, the flavour of which is captured in Luria's emphasis upon the use of language for the planning and control (particularly the self-regulation) of behaviour. The point where the views of many scholars diverge concerns the nature of the interaction between language and other representational systems in the developing child, although most agree in regarding the child's action-patterns as the source of later representational systems and perhaps the focus of their interaction. Thus Piaget [31] maintains that "language is not enough to explain thought, because the structures that characterize thought have their roots in action and sensori-motor mechanisms" and Bruner [5] has hypothesized that play provides the environment of symbolic manipulation necessary for the development of both language and tool-use.

Although little that is precise can be said about the topic, it is clear that the acquisition of language skills can facilitate certain kinds of problem-solving, the acquisition of visuo-spatial skills can facilitate other kinds. It is also possible, as Wales [41] has suggested, that the way in which the pre-school child puts his linguistic knowledge to use may directly impair his performance in certain kinds of perceptual problem-solving commonly known as conservation problems. In other words, the nature of the interaction may not always be to facilitate correct performance.

Considerable importance might attach to asking some of the above questions on a phylogenetic as well as an ontogenetic level. We have previously mentioned the apparent success of two recent attempts to teach language-like communication systems to chimpanzees. In one case, the chimpanzee is taught to manipulate plastic 'word' symbols in structured and referentially appropriate sequences [33]; in the other a variant of American sign-language is being taught [12]. Much scholastic blood is currently being spilled in the debate over whether these chimpanzees are *really* acquiring a 'language'. So far, most of the discussion has ranged around syntactic and semantic issues [4, 25]. It would perhaps be profitable to place more emphasis on the *functions* which the communication-systems serve. In the facilitative and inhibitory interactions of different representational systems we can see more clearly the constraints upon and uses of the ability to manipulate notational devices 'in the head'. It is not a little surprising that avowed Behaviourists, in teaching these chimpanzees their 'languages', should so far have failed to ask directly what utility (or otherwise) the acquisition of these communication-systems might have for other aspects of their subjects' behavioural capacities. What use is a language if all you can do with it is chat to the experimenter? Only by asking questions of this nature will it be possible to establish a biological framework in which the formal characteristics of the chimpanzees' acquired communication-systems are worth comparing with human systems.

De Laguna [9] asserted: "The evolution of language is characterized by a progressive freeing of speech from dependence on the perceived conditions under which it is uttered and heard, and from the behaviour which accompanies it." We have tried in this paper to demonstrate that her assertion is an empirical hypothesis, and we have indicated some of the ways in which current research might be brought to bear upon it. To do this is, in effect, to study pragmatics as defined by Morris.

MRC Speech and Communication Unit, Edinburgh,
and the Department of Psychology of the
University of Edinburgh, Great Britain

BIBLIOGRAPHY

[1] Beth, E. and Piaget, J.: 1964, *Mathematical Epistemology and Psychology*, Reidel, Dordrecht.
[2] Bogen, J. E.: 1969, 'The Other Side of the Brain. II: An Appositional Mind', *Bulletin of the Los Angeles Neurological Societies* 34, 135–162.
[3] Bossert, W. H. and Wilson, E. O.: 1963, 'The Analysis of Olfactory Communication among Animals', *Journal of Theoretical Biology* 5, 443–469.
[4] Brown, R.: 1970, 'The First Sentences of Child and Chimpanzee', in *Psycholinguistics: Selected Papers by Roger Brown*, Free Press, New York.
[5] Bruner, J.: 1972, 'Nature and Uses of Immaturity', *American Psychologist* 27, 1–22.
[6] Chomsky, N.: 1968, *Language and Mind*, Harper and Row, New York.
[7] Chomsky, N.: 1969, 'Linguistics and Philosophy', in S. Hook (ed.), *Language and Philosophy*, New York University Press, New York.
[8] Clark, H., Carpenter, P., and Just, M.: 1973, 'On the Meeting of Semantics and Perception', in W. Chase (ed.), *Visual Information Processing*, Academic Press, New York.
[9] De Laguna, G.: 1927, *Speech: Its Function and Development*, Yale University Press, New Haven.
[10] Firbas, J.: 1964, 'On Defining the Theme in Functional Sentence Analysis', *Travaux linguistiques de Prague* 1, 267–280.

[11] Gainotti, G.: 1972, 'Emotional Behaviour and Hemispheric Side of Lesion', *Cortex* **8**, 41–55.

[12] Gardner, B. and Gardner, R.: 1971, 'Two-Way Communication with an Infant Chimpanzee', in A. Schrier and F. Stollnitz (eds.), *Behaviour of Non-human Primates*, Vol. IV, Academic Press, New York.

[13] Geschwind, N.: 1964, 'The Development of the Brain and the Evolution of Language', *Monograph Series on Languages and Linguistics* **17**, 155–169.

[14] Geschwind, N.: 1969, 'Anatomy and the Higher Functions of the Brain', in R. S. Cohen and M. W. Wartofsky (eds.), *Boston Studies in the Philosophy of Science*, Reidel, Dordrecht.

[15] Gombrich, E. H.: 1972, 'The Visual Image', *Scientific American* **227**, 82–96.

[16] Halliday, M. A. K.: 1970, 'Language Structures and Language Function', in J. Lyons (ed.), *New Horizons in Linguistics*, Penguin Books, Harmondsworth.

[17] Herder, J. G.: 1772, *Ursprung der Sprache*, Akademie Verlag, Berlin.

[18] Hewes, G.: 1970, 'New Light on the Gestural Origin of Language', Paper read at the *69th Annual Meeting of the American Anthropological Association*, San Diego, California.

[19] Johnson-Laird, P.: 1968, 'The Choice of the Passive Voice in a Communicative Task', *British Journal of Psychology* **59**, 7–15.

[20] Kuno, S.: 1972, 'Functional Sentence Perspective', *Linguistic Inquiry* **3**, 269–320.

[21] Levy, J.: 1969, 'Possible Basis for the Evolution of Lateral Specialization of the Human Brain', *Nature* **224**, 614–615.

[22] Luria, A. R.: 1961, *The Role of Speech in the Regulation of Normal and Abnormal Behaviour*, Pergamon, Oxford.

[23] Marler, P.: 1970, 'A Comparative Approach to Vocal Learning: Song Development in the White-Crowned Sparrow', *Journal of Comparative and Physiological Psychology, Monograph Section* **71**, 1–25.

[24] Marler, P., Kreith, M., and Tamura, M.: 1962, 'Song Development in Hand-Raised Oregon Juncos', *Auk.* **79**, 12–30.

[25] Marshall, J. C.: 1971, 'Can Humans Talk?', in J. Morton (ed.), *Biological and Social Factors in Psycholinguistics*, Logos Press, London.

[26] Marshall, J. C.: 1973, 'Language, Learning and Laterality', in R. A. and J. S. Hinde (eds.), *Constraints on Learning: Limitations and Preconditions*, Academic Press, London.

[27] Milner, B.: 1967, 'Discussion', in C. H. Millikan and F. L. Darley (eds.), *Brain Mechanisms Underlying Speech and Language*, Grune and Stratton, New York.

[28] Morris, C.: 1946, *Signs, Language and Behaviour*, Prentice-Hall, New York.

[29] Nash, R.: 1970, 'John Likes Mary more than Bill', *Phonetica* **22**, 170–188.

[30] Nottebohn, F.: 1972, 'The Origins of Vocal Learning', *The American Naturalist* **106**, 116–140.

[31] Piaget, J.: 1967, *Six Psychological Studies*, Random House, New York.

[32] Posner, M.: 1969, 'Abstraction and the Process of Recognition', in J. Spence and G. Bowers (eds.), *The Psychology of Learning and Motivation*, Vol. III, Academic Press, New York.

[33] Premack, D.: 1971, 'Some General Characteristics of a Method for Teaching Language to Organisms that do not Ordinarily Acquire it', in L. E. Jarrard (ed.), *Cognitive Processes of Nonhuman Primates*, Academic Press, New York.

[34] Pribram, K.: 1971, *Languages of the Brain*, Prentice-Hall, Englewood Cliffs, New Jersey.

[35] Ressler, R. H., Cialdini, R. B., Ghoca, M. L., and Kleist, S. M.: 1968, 'Alarm Pheromone in the Earthworm Lumbricus Terrestis', *Science* **161**, 597–599.
[36] Ryan, J.: 1974, 'Early Language Development: Towards a Communicational Analysis', in M. P. M. Richards (ed.), *The Integration of the Child in the Social World*, Cambridge University Press, London.
[37] Steinthal, C.: 1855, *Grammatik, Logik und Psychologie*, Dümmler, Berlin.
[38] Terzian, H. and Ceccotto, C.: 1959, 'Su un nuovo metodo per la determinazione e lo studio della dominanza emisferica', *Giorn. Psichiat. Neuropat.* **87**, 889–924.
[39] Vygotsky, L. S.: 1962, *Thought and Language*, MIT Press, Cambridge, Mass.
[40] Wales, R. J.: 1971, 'Comparing and Contrasting', in J. Morton (ed.), *Biological and Social Factors in Psycholinguistics*, Logos Press, London.
[41] Wales, R. J.: 1973, 'The Child's Sentences Make Sense of the World', in F. Bresson and J. Mehler (eds.), *Les Problèmes Actuelles de Psycholinguistique*, CNRS, Paris.
[42] Wason, P. C.: 1965, 'The Contexts of Plausible Denial', *J. Verb. Learn. Verb. Behav.* **4**, 7–11.

ISAAK REVZIN

FROM ANIMAL COMMUNICATION TO
HUMAN SPEECH

*An Attempt at a Semiotic Analysis of the Problems of the
Origins of Language**

The problem of the origin of language has been considered anew in each
epoch from various standpoints and the results are rather discouraging.
Today one can hardly be optimistic enough to postulate its eventual
solution. However, this should not lead to the complete exclusion of this
question from the range of problems which a linguist may profitably
study.

The need to return to this problem is dictated by the following considerations:

(1) The extension of the semiotic point of view to the phenomenon
of language, which has helped to uncover a number of new aspects, not
previously considered nor properly evaluated.

(2) The development of the theory of universals, leading to definition
of several properties of human language, distinct from known systems
of animal communication.

(3) The birth of 'zoo-semiotics' and the consequent blow to the myth
that no language may exist within the animal world.

We shall be considering in detail each of these points.

I. SEMIOTIC CONCEPTS

Analysis of the functions of language has made it possible to separate
the following two properties: (a) Sign-designatum, i.e. an object or a
property existing in the real world. (b) Sign-content (or 'meaning'), i.e.
the totality of relations established by means of language between the
various designata, and between the speaker and the designata.

In its turn, the concept of 'content' can be further subdivided into:
(1) *periphrastic content*, i.e. that invariant component of content of a given
sign, surviving its translation within the limits of a given language, or
into another language; and (2) *form-bound content*, connected with a
particular description of a designatum in a given language which may
be lost through translation.

Form-bound content can either be *cognitive*, i.e. connected with a

C. Cherry (ed.), Pragmatic Aspects of Human Communication, 15–26. All Rights Reserved
Copyright © 1974 by D. Reidel Publishing Company, Dordrecht-Holland

certain thought or concept independent of the act of communication, or *communicative*, i.e. reflecting some relation between the speaker, the listener, and the message being uttered (here we will find the concepts of time, person, subjective modality, and also the attributes connected with the location of the participants in a given act of communication).

Another distinction of importance in our discussion is that between the sign-type, and its specimens (the latter being sometimes referred to as sign-events). And the third is that between iconic, indexal, and symbolic signs.

II. CONCERNING THE UNIVERSALS

In his formulation of language universals Hockett [1] has listed a number of general features which, in his opinion, distinguish a real language from communication-systems used by animals. Among these are:

(1) The vocal-auditory channel.

(2) The rapid fading (all language signals are evanescent).

(3) The interchangeability – the same person incorporating both the transmitter and the receiver.

(4) The arbitrariness of a sign.

(5) The discrete nature of an utterance.

(6) The 'displacement' property – messages may refer to objects removed in space and in time from the locality and the instant of a given utterance.

(7) The openness of linguistic communication – the possibility of creation of new linguistic messages.

(8) The structural duality of patterning (constructions of meaningful units out of elements bearing no meaning themselves).

(9) Prevarication (the possibility of false or meaningless messages).

This list suggests that gradual acquisition of these features may postulate an evolutionary mechanism. We shall attempt to deal with some of its aspects.

III. BASIC FACTS GAINED FROM ZOO-SEMIOTICS

Rapid development of the subject of Zoo-semiotics leads to an almost monthly appearance of new discoveries, forcing one to reconsider many anthropocentric views. We shall select a few only of the experimental data, bearing directly upon the matter in hand.

(1) As the Gardners have shown [2], the chimpanzee can easily learn a communication system based upon gesture. They are capable, by its means, of attaining symbolic generalization, and can show a certain syntactic productivity, etc.

(2) Despite the generally held belief, that synesthesic phenomena appear only with man [3], the latest experiments with chimpanzee and orang-outang have indicated that they are able to associate information received via different channels.

(3) These apes are capable of performing quite complex operations, being able to remember coded sequences and probabilities of one signal following another [5]. In other words they perceive 'speech' as a Markov-process.

It is reasonable to assume that the ancestors of man possessed intellectual abilities of a degree not lower than that of the present-day apes. Hence one may postulate that they too had similar skills. In other words one may assume that human language derived from a reasonably well-developed communication system. We can, therefore, visualise the birth of language, as a 'hominization' process [6] of a certain code or codes of signals, which we may call a 'proto-tongue'.

A. The Role of 'Fascination' in the System of 'Proto-Tongue'

Knorosov, when dealing with the general theory of communication, has introduced a very fruitful concept of 'fascination' [7]. By this term he meant that signal component which serves to convey the will of the speaker to the listener, but does not contain within itself any of the basic information. In other words, this signal component influences the listener to receive the information in the manner desired by the originator of the message. According to Knorosov, 'fascination' plays a very important part in communication among the animal groups hierarchically structured.

Ethnology tells us that the hierarchical structure among groups of higher apes is delineated with very great precision (Chauvin [8]). On the other hand, we also know that emotional-fascination signals in the midst of such groups are, as a rule, transmitted by the voice (see the detailed description of such signals in the work of Ladygina-Kots [9]).

Hence it seems natural to assume that in the proto-tongue also, the fascination component of the message was voice-transmitted. The vocal-auditory channel is particularly well adapted to transmitting fascination signals, since it can cope with a continuous alteration of the parameters of a signal in two independent directions (a) from high to low, and (b) from saturated to unsaturated. Psychology tells us that these parameters are of the highest synesthesical significance.

It is unlikely that in the initial stages the fascination component was separated from the judgement component, concerning objects and actions, alluded to within the message. In a hierarchical society the privilege of ethical judgements of the type desirable/undesirable seems to be inseparable from the will of the originator of the fascination signal, i.e. the highest member of the hierarchy.

B. The Primordial Communication System

For the second component of the 'proto-tongue' one may suggest a system of signals indicating the orientation of objects relative to the initiator of the message and its receiver. Here one can expect to find the concepts conveyed in modern language by words of the type 'here', 'there', 'near', 'distant', and by different grammatical categories etc.

It is obvious that such a system, especially when reinforced by fascination signals, is sufficient for communication in the 'language of things', for these signals induce a definite syntax upon the set of objects. The resulting orderliness makes this set a carrier of some degree of information dealing with 'now' and 'here'.

If the fascination signals were likely to have been continuous in nature, the deictic (i.e. indicating) signals which we are now discussing must have been discrete. Hence it is reasonable to assume that initially communicative signals were given by means of gesticulation. Here we are in agreement with Wundt [15], who has postulated a primordial gesture language. We also think that sounds were originally used to express feeling (if 'fascination' is included), while gestures were employed to express concepts (though we limit the primordial function of gesture to deixis only).

C. The System of Permanent (Long Duration) Signals

For the third component of the proto-tongue one may visualise a system of permanent signals, of the nature of marks such as cuts, notches etc. Such signals may have been either purely utilitarian in execution, without any aesthetic function (such as were still used in the 19th century by illiterate peasants in Russia) or, alternatively, true works of art, e.g. in cave and rock paintings [11].

D. General Features of the Proto-Tongue

Thus we can characterize the proto-tongue as consisting of three different types of signal, transmitted along three separate channels. Parallel utilization of several separate channels is characteristic of animal communication in general (e.g. the co-existence of voice and chemical (odour) signalling among wolves). From the purely semiotic point of view each of the three systems can be described as iconic. Thus:

(a) A 'fascination' voice signal is based on association with feeling (synesthesia) (e.g. the unpleasantness of a shrill, or the exaltation of a saturated tone).

(b) The iconic nature of deictic (indicating) signals, even in present-day language, was pointed out by Jakobson [12]. More precisely Jakobson considers that these signs, in a language of the modern type, combine within themselves to have the nature of sign-symbols (i.e. signs conventionally related to the objects they are representing) and sign-indices. The gesture signals of the proto-tongue are either directly associated with an object, or the object is associated with a projection of these signs.

(c) Things, employed in an utterance as signs, are obviously iconic, being signs of themselves. Cuts, notches, etc. and subsequently drawings are also iconic.

Thus the 'arbitrariness' of the sign, which Hockett considers as one of the basic characters of a language, is absent from the proto-tongue; also absent is the character of 'duality'. Duality of patterning is by no means characteristic of iconic systems.

Other characters due to Hockett hold for some systems but not for others. None of them is valid simultaneously for the fascination and communicative systems (if one disregards the very secondary nature of the phenomenon of fading; which latter in its turn is invalid for the third system).

IV. THE CRUCIAL STAGE: COALESCENCE OF THE THREE SYSTEMS

The crucial stage in the development of language from the proto-tongue was the coalescence of the three systems, initially separate, into one. The period of transition must have been a lengthy one, the development passing through a number of intermediate stages.

A. Appearance of a Sign-Response to a Sign-Stimulus

We have assumed that for each of the systems of the 'proto-tongue' there was some kind of active response to each of the signs. But at a certain stage of the development it could have happened that, to a sign stimulus in one of the systems, the response became itself another sign, perhaps from another system.

B. Synchronization of the Three Systems

It is logical to assume a body of magic or worship-like actions, probably originating within the upper strata of the hierarchy, directed towards the establishment of correspondence between the signals of the three systems. This could have created the possibility of sign substitution when conveying a given message (earlier, as we have pointed out, signs of a given system referred to a particular sphere).

C. Location of All of the Three Systems within a Single Channel

This must have been the video-auditory channel, the remaining channels becoming redundant. The system of permanent signs assumed the form of 'proto-writing'. Vendryès [13] and Van Ginneken [14] think that picto-grammic writing may have preceded the voice, which is in agreement with the scheme of development here suggested.

D. Weakening of the 'Fascination' Aspect of the Voice

This process could have brought about the character called by Hockett 'interchangeability'. Besides, there could have been already a number of possible responses to a given sign. Thus, a sign was assuming truly 'human' significance, linked with a full freedom of choice. To this stage it is also possible to ascribe the separation of an 'individual' from the body of the 'group' – the appearance of communicative contrast between 'I' and 'not I'.

At a further stage in the development, the free choice of response-signs could have brought about the character named 'prevarication' by Hockett.

E. Transfer of a Reduced 'Fascination' Value to the New Voice Signal

Such signals, being voice-translations of gestures or 'permanent' signals, would still have had such colouration. In this case the signal form, in particular the choice of one or another acoustic parameter, must have had from the very beginning an effect on the meaning conveyed. Here one might find an explanation of the appearance of a real human phenomenon – that of 'inner form', or in a broader context, of form-bound meaning (sense, content).

The mechanism connecting sound with meaning was determined either by the fascination element, or by a value judgement of an object being reflected in an appropriate world model. In some cases one may assume a more random connection between meaning and fascination or value judgement. Such a mechanism could have been particularly useful, as it would have tended to involve a progressively larger number of designata.

In a later stage of the evolutionary process the 'fascination/judgement' factors, having acted as catalysts ('starting mechanisms'), would have become mere invocational or poetical formulae, no longer essential as means of communication. Nevertheless, the principles of attaining inner meaning by vocal means could have remained, gradually transforming themselves into a purely intellectual phenomenon – that of form-bound content.

The transition to a unified system, utilizing only the vocal-auditory channel, had also some other consequences. Disregarding here the purely physiological factors influencing the development of this channel as well as the feedback of this development on the available means of a sound language (this question is treated in depth in the work of Baudouin de Courtenay [6]) we would wish to call attention to some purely semiotic consequences of this transition.

The Wundt-theory already deals with the most important distinction between the 'indicative' (hinweisend) and the 'imitative' gesture [15]. Cassirer [16] has pointed out that this distinction is even more important during the period of transition to the sound-language, where the sound-imitative element always kept a secondary place.

Consider, in this connection, the number of unsatisfactory attempts to derive the origins of speech from mere sound-imitation; nevertheless, some of the papers, e.g. that of Gasov-Ginzburg [17], contain interesting material.

A speech-sign does not represent an object (just as it is not represented by voice in the 'proto-tongue'), but rather it translated, into the sound-code, the concept of that object. The theory of sound-imitation is unable to explain the origin of the basic character of human speech, namely its duality.

On the other hand the structuring of a speech-sign from phonemes without meaning in modern language (though they need not necessarily be void of meaning, as pointed out by Shcherba and his followers [18]), can be a consequence of the combination of fascination, communicative, and denotative signals, each of which may have had some meaning by itself.

Though we cannot consider sound-imitation to be a basic vocal (glot-togonic) principle, its secondary effects could have been quite consider-able. Vyacheslav Ivanov [10] has shown that in many unrelated lan-guages an object is often described by the sound it makes. The impor-tance of this class of description is convincingly argued by him, under-lining the special attention paid in ancient human communities to the sound elements of the language. This demonstration is in complete agreement with our hypothesis concerning the initial fascination role of the voice.

The transition towards a unified system, where the voice was used to transmit not only fascination but also denotative and communicative meanings, may have had another important consequence. Earlier, when a communicative gesture related an idea to an object as a permanent signal, the object itself played a part in the communication process. But, subsequently, when the denotative function was transferred to a voice-produced symbol, the communicative signal carrying the meaning of 'this', 'here', 'now' related not to an object, but to a certain sign-sample (a sign-event). It is exactly because of this, that it became possible to express ideas connected with the concepts of 'this particular sign-sample', or 'this particular sign-sequence' (for example, the meaning of 'I' to which we referred earlier).

Already in the proto-tongue stage there must have existed the possi-bility of identifying various sign-events with a certain basic sign-type. At the more advanced stage there appeared a feature making it possible to distinguish, in a given communicative situation, between a sign accompanied by a communicative signal and a sign-type given by the same voice signal but void of the communicative component. This could have brought about the facility of generalization by means of speech.

V. HYPOTHESIS CONCERNING THE ORIGIN OF DUAL PATTERNING

The translation of gesture as a deictic sign into the voice-auditory code could have passed through an intermediate stage of the 'vocal gesture' (e.g. concave or convex lip position). Such vocal gestures could have led to the appearance of segmentation.

We know from typology of languages that the most general form of word structure (or the analogous binomial in languages like Chinese) has the shape $(A) + B + (A')$. The grammatical elements (deictic and communicative, in the greater majority of cases) are contained within the A and A' terms, while the B-term contains the denotative element, the so called root.

This suggests that this structure is of a very great age, and that the primordial 'word-sentence' had the form: (voice-gesture) + denotative signal + (voice-gesture).

From what has been said earlier, it follows that the denotative signal was voice-transmitted, as the coalescence of the fascination and the denotative components of the signal must have already occurred, while the communicative component was conveyed by means of the voice-gesture. Broadly speaking the meaning conveyed could correspond to some such formula as 'this house here'.

It is possible to propose another step, somewhat more hypothetical perhaps, but still within bounds of probability, by identifying the voice-gesture with proto-consonants (click-like sound complexes with dominant noise), and the denotative component with voice dominant proto-vowels.

This hypothesis suggests a comparison between the primordial phrase and primordial syllable. It makes it possible to interpret an observation due to Kurylowycz [19], that the syllable and phrase structures are isomorphic, as an echo from the relations which were significant in the most remote times.

Our hypothesis does not exclude the possibility that some such complexes might have been sound-imitative in nature. This is particularly likely in cases where the presence of the fascination component sharpened their symbolic power. Of special significance is the fact that the signal was perceived as a unified whole, quite independently of the meaning of its separate components.

This process comparable to idiom formation, familiar to us at various stages of development of languages of modern type, can be justified by arguments advanced by Information Theory. Frequently-occurring coding sequences are advantageously replaced by a single sign in some newly devised alphabet, particularly if one considers the importance of the time factor to the ancestors of modern man, when transmitting messages of importance. Thus the process of idiom formation is possibly responsible for the dual nature of codification of human speech – by means of phonemes on one hand, and by means of morphemes (and later words) on the other.

Another idea advanced by Knorosov appears fruitful in suggesting a possible further development. He has called attention to the fact that one can build up a fairly rich language from only a small number of proto-syllables. Structurally its word-formation consists of combination of pairs of proto-syllables. If primary idiomatic process is allowed for, it guards against undue expenditure of proto-syllables, and allows a sharp increase in the available roots (simple doubling is known from signalling within the animal kingdom).

As a result of this doubling process, the vowels of each part began to influence one another, possibly reducing their original fascination content. But the sound-imitating doubled roots, especially if the two parts were identical, tended to keep their original fascination value. This is known from many languages (e.g. the Semitic and the Altaic-tongues).

The idiom process has further reduced the initial significance of the constituent parts. The proto-vowels and proto-consonants were transformed into phonemes, with the consequent loss of their ancient meanings. Thus the system of dual-articulation based on the phonemes, a unit distinct from the morpheme, has made its appearance. Doubling could also assist the differentiation between denotative and communicative elements at this or a further stage of development. Many linguists have noticed that roots can, as a rule, be reduced to bi-syllabic units, while grammatical elements (i.e. deictic, and, later on, other communicative elements) are usually mono-syllabic in structure.

VI. A HYPOTHESIS CONCERNING RECURSIVITY

The distillation of the communicative elements, and the possibility of their further subdivision into two classes, classifying, or actualizing on one hand, and relating to the speaker and to the time of utterance on the other, make it possible to construct a sentence containing subject and verb.

The freedom with which these indicators may characterize an object or an action leads to a description of an action not unlike that of an object, when localizing modifiers are used. The appearance of recursivity follows naturally, one phrase being placed within another. Some scholars [20] consider the phenomenon of recursivity as a basic distinction between human speech and animal communication; animal communication can be described by a Markov-process. Such a process is capable of describing certain features of human speech, but not that of recursivity.

Hence one is led to suggest that the original appearance of this character may have been caused by the combination of communicative and denotative means. And to this combination, according to our hypothesis, the creation of human speech is mainly due.

Institut Slavjanovedenija,
Sovietskoj Akademii Nauk, Moscow, U.S.S.R.

NOTE

* Translated from the Russian by D. Rutenberg, Imperial College, London, (April 1973).

BIBLIOGRAPHY

[1] Ch. F. Hockett, 'The Problem of Universals in Language', in *Universals in Language* (ed. by J. Greenberg), MIT Press, Cambridge, Massachusetts, 1963.
[2] A. R. Gardner and B. T. Gardner, 'Teaching Sign Language to a Chimpanzee', *Science* (1969) 664.
[3] Jane B. Lancaster, 'Primitive Communication Systems and the Emergence of Human Language', in *Primates* (ed. by C. Jay), New York 1968.
[4] R. K. Davenport and C. M. Rogers, 'Intermodal Equivalence of Stimuli in Apes', *Science* (1970) 279.

[5] Peter C. Reynolds, 'Evolution of Primitive Vocal-Auditory Communication Systems', *American Anthropologist* **70** (1968) 300.

[6] I. A. Baudouin de Courtenay, 'One of the Factors of Gradual Hominization of Phonology of Speech as seen from the Point of View of Anthropology', in *Izbrannÿe Trudÿ po Obshchemu Yazÿkoznanyu*, Vol. II, Moscow 1963 (*Selected Papers on General Linguistics*).

[7] Yu. V. Knorozov. The Theory of 'Fascination' proposed by Knorozov has not appeared in published form. Reference to it is made by M. I. Burlakova in the book *Strukturno-tipologicheskie Issledovanya*, Moscow 1962, p. 285 (*Researches into the Structure and Typology of Language*).

[8] R. Chauvin, *Les Sociétés Animales de L'Abeille au Gorille*, Paris 1963.

[9] N. N. Ladygina-Kots, appendix to the book by Jan Dembovski, *Psychology of Apes*, Moscow 1973.

[10] Vyacheslav Ivanov, 'Suffix* -sk- > Baltic–šk–and the Problem of Verbs Denoting Sounds', in *Donum Balticum* (Festschrift für Chr. S. Stang) Stockholm 1970, p. 206.

[11] Collected papers: *Rannie formÿ iskusstva* (*Early art forms*), Moscow 1972. Papers by A. D. Solyar, V. N. Toporov, Vyacheslav Vsevold Ivanov and others.

[12] R. Jakobson, *Shifters, Verbal Categories and the Russian Verb*, Harvard University 1957.

[13] J. Vendryès, *Le Langage*, Paris 1921.

[14] Jac. van Ginneken, 'Ein neuer Versuch zur Typologie der Älteren Sprachstrukturen', *Travaux du Cercle Linguistique de Prague*, No. 8, Prague 1939.

[15] W. Wundt, *Völkerpsychologie*, Vol. I: *Die Sprache* (2nd ed.), Leipzig 1904.

[16] E. Cassirer, *Philosophie der Symbolischen Formen*, Part I: *Die Sprache*, Berlin 1923.

[17] A. M. Gazov-Ginzburg, *Bÿl li Jasyk Isobrasitelen v Svoichi stokakh?* (*Was the Nature of Language Figurative at Its Origins; Evidence of the Pre-Semitic Roots*), Moscow 1965.

[18] E.g. see L. R. Zinder, *Obschaya Fonetika*, Leningrad 1958 (*General Phonetics*).

[19] J. Kurylowicz, 'Contribution à la Theorie de la Syllable', in *Esquisses Linguistiques*, Wroclaw-Krakow 1960.

[20] Jane H. Hill, 'On the Evolutionary Foundations of Language', *American Anthropologist* **74** (1972).

DENNIS DICKS

EXPERIMENTS WITH EVERYDAY CONVERSATION

I. INTRODUCTION

Most of us can ride a bicycle, swim, and write our own language. In one sense, we 'know' how to do these things, for they are part of our wealth of acquired skills. In another sense, we do not 'know' these activities, because we cannot explicitly describe how we perform them. When someone asks 'how do you write with a pen ?', we usually reply 'like this', and give a demonstration. If the question were asked over an ordinary telephone, a verbal explication would be exceedingly difficult. Our 'knowledge' of these skills is intuitive, rather than scientific.

For our social skills, this is even more the case. Almost all humans can speak a language (those who cannot are universally assumed to be physically or mentally defective, even in the absence of any other symptoms). But an explanation of how we generate utterances or how we understand them is still beyond us all. An event as common as everyday conversation remains much more inscrutable than the other side of the moon.

There are many reasons for our ignorance. For one thing, social interaction is much more intractable than simple physical phenomena, like spheres rolling down inclines: we cannot easily remove the event from its usual setting without destroying it. Spheres and inclines and all the paraphernalia of physics are inanimate, and cannot refuse to perform if we change their mass or slope. We cannot manipulate humans as easily – and, furthermore, in observing them, we are necessarily participating in the very event we wish to describe! On one hand, our presence as observers changes the nature of the event. On the other hand, our explicit description depends upon our implicit understanding of this activity. For instance, if we want to examine the organisation of a vocal utterance, a simple record of the speech sounds (as provided by a phonetic analysis or a frequency spectrogram) is not adequate. A phonemic analysis, reflecting the boundaries of words and phrases, is more appropriate to

C. Cherry (ed.), Pragmatic Aspects of Human Communication, 27–50. All Rights Reserved
Copyright © 1974 by D. Reidel Publishing Company, Dordrecht-Holland

this end. But, for the moment, we cannot provide the scientific specifications for a machine which will distinguish a complete phonemic phrase ('he gave the book') from an incomplete one ('he gave the book to'). Here, the human observer is our only instrument.

Analysis of social interaction has been hampered by several difficulties with method. In the telephone industry, for instance, the millions of daily conversations (precisely the sample which system-planners are interested in studying) cannot be ethically tapped. Consequently, attempts have been made to 'model' interaction by having people perform some task: interview one another, play a game, solve a problem.

Modelling of interaction is also encouraged by the diversity of social events. Intent upon quantifying behaviour, social scientists have attempted to control the motives of their sample populations through the use of standard tasks, such as the interview or game. When this is the case, the impulse to interact, and the goals of interaction, are imposed upon the participants. They are thus 'extrinsically' motivated. Conceivably, interaction under this type of circumstance may differ from that occurring when the motives for interaction are 'intrinsic' to the participants and their momentary situation. For contrast, let us call this latter type of interaction *natural* conversation.

An additional problem is that the crusade for quantification in the social sciences has led many researchers to rely upon types of 'concrete' data: message frequency, speech levels, numbers of words spoken, scores on questionnaires. In some cases, the most accessible datum may be the most relevant to the research goal (for example, level of speech is relevant in assessing the quality of telephone systems); but in other cases, the use of similar data may lead to over-simplification (for example, use of number-of-words-spoken as an index of the psychological aspects of everyday speech; Krause, 1969). Even if the context of social interaction were to be standardised, each participant would still bring his own perceptual experience to the meeting. It would be too optimistic to hope to describe the resultant social intercourse by means of a single dependent variable.

That social interaction is a complex phenomenon is news to no one. What can we do about studying it? Give up?

To begin with, let us not assume that our experimental models-games in particular are adequate reflections of reality. Games are designed to standardise only one antecedent condition for conversation: its purpose as perceived by the participants. The goal of the game becomes the focus of interaction. And to some extent, the rules of the game determine the actual content of the conversation. But perhaps there is no parallel with everyday conversation, where the goals and rules are not extrinsic, not explicitly recognised nor agreed upon by the conversants. Even simulations, such as management-decision games, are only adequate models for some situations, wherein the 'cause' of the conversation (expanding sales, for example) is directly related to the content of the social exchange ('let's advertise more').

Another aspect of social interaction is its physical setting. A doctor's office will normally lead to different types of exchange than will a barber's shop. In themselves, these two settings generate different types of social expectations. If someone in a white coat enters the office, a man sitting there might say, 'I've got this pain right here'. The statement might not be as appropriate under similar circumstances in a barber's shop.

However, if another man entered the doctor's office in attire similar to his own, the seated man might ask, 'What time is your appointment?' His behaviour reflects his perception of the newcomer as another patient rather than the doctor. The participants' group affinity is a third aspect of social interaction.

Obviously, these three facets of the interpersonal situation (and others) interact to determine its content. Subtle cues to the purpose of a meeting probably lie in the size of the meeting place, the arrangement of chairs or other furniture or equipment, and in the ambient levels of light and sound. Group affinity encompasses many facets of person-perception: sex, race, age, language group, occupation, religion, political and other affiliations, all of which contribute to the participants' expectations of what will happen at a meeting.

But these three types of conditions are amenable to a certain degree of control for experimental purposes. Physical setting can be altered through the construction of special environments – a sort of experimental architecture. Group affinity can be manipulated by selecting the participants; the goals and rules of interaction too by imposition of different types of extrinsic task – or by allowing the interplay of the participants' intrinsic motives. Therefore, a type of 'natural experiment' on conversation becomes feasible.

In a 'natural experiment', a process which occurs naturally is induced under the observer's microscope, while a few of the purportedly key factors are manipulated. Since a demonstration may outweigh a thousand protestations, the next Section begins an account of an experiment which has been performed to induce and examine *natural* conversation.

II. AN EXPERIMENT ON NATURAL CONVERSATION

In order to generate *natural* conversation, it would appear necessary to arrange meetings wherein the 'cause' of the assembly is not related to the nature of social exchange. For instance, this situation probably prevails in a restaurant; people may meet there in the course of nourishing themselves, but their exchange will not be restricted to 'pass the butter', 'have some of this'. Discourse is (generally) even further removed from the cause of the meeting in a public bar or coffee lounge. If people with vaguely compatible group affinities (common language-group is probably the minimal requirement) are brought together in this type of setting, *natural* conversation might be expected to occur – especially if the participants do not have well-defined roles which dominate the interaction (as would be the case if a person sat down and a woman in waitress' attire brought in the coffee).

Let us suppose that control of these factors permits the generation of conversation; what sort of data will lead to fruitful analysis? Words? Postures? Facial expressions? Gestures of the hands? The human participant undoubtedly attends to all of these; they interact to determine the quality and sense of social interaction. Physical and vocal gestures are intrinsically entwined in social behaviour; – communication is an integral performance. Vocal gesture may be transcribed as written language. Physical gesture may also be codified. But this complex task may be simplified by attending to the direction of the participants' eye-glance. Clearly, gestures which are not seen by the other may illustrate the state of one participant to an observer, but they can have no communicative value within the interaction. Moreover, eye-glance not only provides information to the looker, but is in itself a most influential gesture.

In view of the experience of other social scientists (Birdwhistell, 1960; Kendon and Cook, 1969; Schegloff, 1971), it was decided to concentrate on accurately recording the speech and glances of both members of a dyad.[1] A pilot study indicated considerable differences between males and females on these measures, so females were not included in the major project. Besides, the readily available population was the largely-male undergraduate body at a technical university in London, England.

Twelve such undergraduates were contacted as they reposed in a student lounge. Each was asked to participate in a series of three experiments, under the pretext that these involved 'technical assessment of a video-telephone', for a modest payment ($37\frac{1}{2}$ NP. per session). Each was requested to bring a friend to the first session.

The true purpose of the experiment was not revealed, at this stage.

At this first session, the student and his friend were asked to fill in the FIRO-B inventory of interpersonal behaviour. Then they were ushered into what appeared to be a small coffee lounge and asked to relax while the experimenter prepared his equipment. The experimenter then left the room.

In fact, the coffee room had been carefully pre-arranged, being laid out to facilitate social interaction. Only two chairs, of heavy and comfortable construction so as to discourage movement, were in the room; these chairs were placed about five feet apart, at right angles to one another to encourage pleasant confrontation (Sommer, 1959). Books and other articles which might have distracted the conversants were removed.

A mock-up video-telephone was in evidence in this coffee room. At the outset, its picture screen was blank, but its television camera silently viewed one participant through a half-silvered mirror. A second camera viewed the other participant through a 'blackboard' made of heavily smoked glass; in this way a full-face image of both participants was available (unknown to them) for video-taping by the experimenter. At the same time, a microphone disguised as a loudspeaker rested near the elbow of each conversant (Figures 1 and 2).

The *natural* conversation of the two students was taped over the initial five-minute period (Period P 1). Then the experimenter returned, commented that the equipment was ready, and turned on the video-telephone screen. He then lead participant X (Figure 1) to the second video-telephone terminal, located in the next room. After a short practice on the devices, the participants were asked to play the Deutsch-Krause Trucking game (Figure 3)[2], over the video-telephone.

Play was allowed to continue for 10 minutes, although only the first

5 were taped (Period P 2). Then the experimenter asked the students if they wanted coffee. As the answer was almost invariably 'yes', the two cups of coffee were placed on the table in the lounge, thereby obliging participant X to rejoin Y. The two were urged to relax over their coffee, in the lounge, and the experimenter left to surreptitiously record another five-minute sample of *natural* conversation (Period P 3). Finally, the participants were paid and allowed to leave.

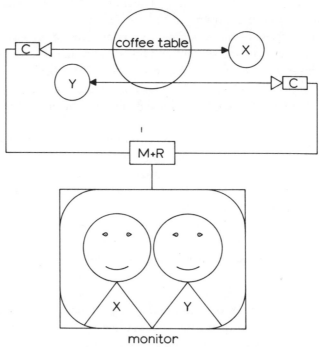

Fig. 1.   Diagram of the 'lounge', seating two subjects, X and Y; the position of the cameras (C) is shown, and the mix- and recording of the video-images is schematically presented (M + R). The output is juxta-posed full-face images of both X and Y (plus sound-track).

The procedure was essentially the same when the participants returned for the second and third sessions; but, in these, the meetings occurred between strangers rather than friends. Pairs of strangers were composed by matching the original participants in new combinations. Compatibility in giving and receiving affection (a measure derived from the FIRO-B scores; Schutz, 1967) was found empirically to be an adequate criterion of 'friendship', and so was used in forming the new pairs. Six of the original pairs showing such compatibility were used in sessions 2 and 3. Only at the end of the sessions were the subjects informed of the true nature of the experiment, for ethical reasons; they were then invited to preside during the erasure of the video-tapes. In fact, no-one accepted the invitation.

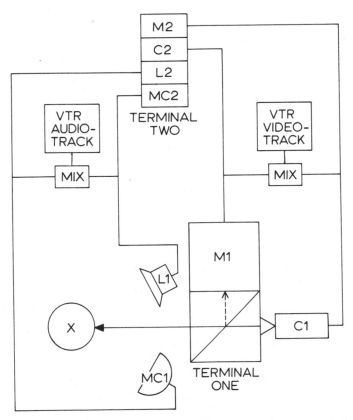

Fig. 2.   Schematic diagram of the video-telephone network. Terminal one is drawn in detail to show how the half-silvered mirror is positioned at 45 degrees to reflect the video-image towards the viewer, X, while allowing the camera to look through this image. The camera's line of regard is indicated by the solid line, the viewer's line of regard by the broken line. The signals from the two terminals are superimposed in the separate mixers, then synchronously recorded on the audio- and video tracks of the same video-taperecorder. C = camera, L = loudspeaker, M = video-monitor, MC = microphone, VTR = video-tape-recorder.

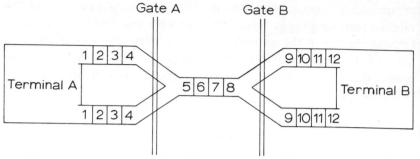

Fig. 3.   The rules and playing surface of the game used in the GAM period, $P\,2$.

Rules

(1) Each player sets out from his own terminal towards the opposite one, and collects an imaginary £ 10 when he reaches it, then he must return to his own terminal before beginning another trip.

(2) The goal is to earn more money than the other player.

(3) Player A begins, the each player moves his own lorry in turn.

(4) Each lorry can move only in the forward direction.

(5) Each move may be 0, 1, or 2 numbered squares.

(6) The gates A and B are controlled respectively by players A and B.

(7) Each player can move freely through his own gate, but must ask for and receive permission of the other player before passing through his gate, in either direction.

(8) The lorries cannot move toward one another on the same road; this causes collision. If collision occurs, both lorries must return to their respective terminals and begin again.

The resultant factorial design with repeated measures is shown in Tables I and II. Factor P (type of interaction) had 3 levels; Factor F (degree of acquaintance) had 2 levels. The intention was to have twelve subjects in each cell of the design (i.e. $n = 12$); however, since two subjects

TABLE I

Representation of a single experimental session. Each pair of students participated in 3 periods of social interaction. In $P2$, the constraints of the Deutsch-Krause Trucking Game were imposed upon interaction by the experimenter. In $P1$ and $P3$, no constraints were imposed by the experimenter

Period	Type of social interaction
$P1$ or PRE	'Natural conversation'
$P2$ or GAM	Game playing
$P3$ or POS	'Natural conversation'

TABLE II

Representation of the whole experiment. The two independent variables are degree of acquaintance (F) and type of interaction (P). In order to obtain more data on the 2nd level of F, this part of the experiment was replicated. The letters A, B, etc. represent individual students: members of the first 6 pairs participated in 3 separate sessions, with a different partner on each occasion. Because one pair missed the 3rd session, a subset of all the available data was used, to maintain 'within subject' comparisons in the analysis of variance. N = number of pairs participating.

Factor levels		Pairs of students						N
	$P\,1$							
$F\,1$ Friends	$P\,2$	$A\!-\!B$	$C\!-\!D$	$E\!-\!F$	...	$W\!-\!X$		12
	$P\,3$							
	$P\,1$							
$F\,2$	$P\,2$	$A\!-\!D$	$C\!-\!F$	...	$J\!-\!K$			6
	$P\,3$							
Strangers, replicated								
	$P\,1$							
$F\,2$	$P\,2$	$A\!-\!L$	$C\!-\!I$	...	$J\!-\!F$			5
	$P\,3$							

failed to appear in session 3, an n of 9 was used in each cell for the multivariate analysis of variance.

III. ANALYSIS AND DISCUSSION OF THE OUTCOME

In the subsequent analysis of the video-tapes, panels of four observers examined the video-tape of each interaction. One observer attended to the speech of X, pressing a button during the whole time that X talked; another observer similarly pressed a button whilst X looked at Y; and so on. The buttons activated a paper punch, the output of which was subsequently digested by a PDP-15 programme. The programme printed out the cumulative and average duration for each of six variables: X looks at Y $(X\ LK)$; X talks $(X\ TK)$; X looks while Y looks $(X+Y\ LK)$; X talks while Y talks $(X+Y\ TK)$; X looks while talking $(X\ LK+TK)$; and X looks while Y talks $(X\ LK+Y\ TK)$. Here, X stands for either participant in the experiment, and Y stands for his partner. 'Looks' means 'glances at the other conversant', and 'talks' means 'makes any vocal utterance'. For every sample of interaction, two sets of data were

I go to uh three

N I'LL MOVE TO THTHTHREE

uhm   yeah   hang on you're at one now aren't you

I'M AT THREE YEAH I WAS NOW I MOVED TO THREE

ohh   yes   ok ah I'll move to one 'n I collect my ten pounds and

take it back

I'LL MOVE TO FIVE

uhm I'm not going to let you through my gate

OH WELL IN THAT CASE   IN THAT CASE   **** OFF

that's nice isn't it   good god

Y' CAN DO ALL SORTS OF THINGS ON THIS TV IT'S PRETTY GOOD AC-

TUALLY NOW IF THEY CONNECT UP   SORT OF   THE LOCAL BOOKMAKER

AND THINGS YOU KNOW   IT'S IT'S QUITE A GOOD IDEA WELL IT'S

NOT A BAD SYSTEM REALLY QUITE UH IT'S A BIT SORT OF JERRY BUILT

AH   HE'S NOT LISTENING

uhhh   what are y'talking about he's not listening

CAN'T Y' HEAR

yeah vaguely

VAGUELY YEAH IT'S NOT VERY LOUD HAVE T' GET NEARER THE MIKE

yeah

SELL HIM   SELL HIM A MICROPHONE SOMETIME

Fig. 4.   Transcript of the vocal utterances of *X* and *Y*, during GAME. One conversant is indicated by lower case letters, *y*, the other by capitals, *X*. *X* looks at *y* =————; *y* looks at *X* = – – – –. The 'conversational' type of interaction is judged to begin after the **** OFF which ends the game.

obtained by considering each member of the pair in turn. In this way, an accurate record of the temporal coordination of speech and glance was prepared (test/retest reliability: glance = 0.86; speech = 0.86). A complete transcript of the type shown in Figure 4 was also prepared.

To examine differences in behaviour associated with the two factors F and P, multivariate analysis of variance was performed, following the factorial design in Table II. Cumulative and average duration and frequency per minute of the six types of interpersonal event were used as data, after appropriate transformation.

As Table III indicates, degree of acquaintance (Factor F) was not a significant factor. However, statistically significant changes in interper-

TABLE III

Results of multivariate analysis of variance for six events (X looks, X talks, etc.). Data on the cumulative duration, average duration, and frequency of each of these events was used in three separate analyses, each using an F (2 levels of acquaintance) $\times P$ (3 periods) factorial design. The Wilk's Lambda criterion was used as a test of significance, with alpha = 0.05.

Cumulative Duration of six Events

Effect	P
$F \times$ subjects interaction	0.247
$P \times$ subjects interaction	0.069
$F \times P$ interaction	0.548
F main effect	0.666
P main effect	0.039 SIG

Average Duration of six Events

Effect	P
$F \times$ subjects interaction	0.036 SIG
$P \times$ subjects interaction	0.358
$F \times P$ interaction	0.571
F main effect	0.385
P main effect	0.006 SIG

Frequency of six Events

Effect	P
$F \times$ subjects interaction	0.060
$P \times$ subjects interaction	0.356
$F \times P$ interaction	0.128
F main effect	0.782
P main effect	0.002 SIG

sonal behaviour were associated with different types of interaction. In view of this, the effect of factor F on these interpersonal events was not explored in greater detail.

IV. A CLOSER LOOK AT FACTOR P

In the present sample, there was no difference in behaviour between friends and strangers on the set of interaction measures used. There was a difference, for all subjects, between performance in normal conversation (P 1 and P 3) and performance in the game situation (P 2). This difference could be attributed to two facets of the game period: first, interaction in the game period occurred via a video-telephone system rather than face-to-face, as in normal conversation; second, interaction in the

TABLE IV

Results of univariate analysis of variance for each of six variables, with 'game' versus 'natural' behaviour as the lone factor. In this analysis, both samples are drawn from the GAM Period, P 2, as explained in the text. The asterisks signify that variance due to subjects-within-groups is statistically significant at (*) $\alpha = 0.05$, or (**) $\alpha = 0.01$.

	Variable	F	DF	P less than
Cumulative duration	$X\ LK$	20.761	1.7	0.01 SIG
	$X\ TK$	7.265	1.7	0.05 SIG
	$X+Y\ LK$	36.518	1.7	0.01 SIG
	$X+Y\ TK$	4.107	1.7	0.10*
	$X\ LK+TK$	13.871	1.7	0.01 SIG
	$X\ LK+Y\ TK$	13.710	1.7	0.01 SIG
Average duration	$X\ LK$	14.098	1.7	0.01 SIG
	$X\ TK$	7.037	1.7	0.05 SIG
	$X+Y\ LK$	12.009	1.7	0.05 SIG
	$X+Y\ TK$	2.255	1.7	0.25*
	$X\ LK+TK$	8.405	1.7	0.05 SIG
	$X\ LK+Y\ TK$	5.893	1.7	0.05 SIG
Frequency min^{-1}	$X\ LK$	0.246	1.7	
	$X\ TK$	1.432	1.7	
	$X+Y\ LK$	6.725	1.7	0.05 SIG
	$X+Y\ TK$	4.795	1.7	0.10**
	$X\ LK+TK$	5.811	1.7	0.05 SIG
	$X\ LK+Y\ TK$	5.305	1.7	0.10

game period was constrained by the rules and objectives of the game, rather than by the conditions of normal conversation. Fortunately, it was possible to differentiate between these two alternatives by closely examining the period. Some of the participants lost interest in the game, as they played it for the second or third time. After a few minutes of play, they opened a more *natural* dialogue, via the video-telephone. The two types of interaction, game playing and natural conversation, seemed to the intuitive eye, very different in transcript (see Figure 4).

Sessions wherein both types of interaction occurred between the same two people necessarily involved strangers, because of the experimental design. Video-tapes of four such sessions were re-examined: four samples of each type were measured by a panel of observers, as described earlier.

TABLE V

Results of univariate analysis of variance for each of six variables. Here, the one-way analysis distinguishes *natural* behaviour occurring during the GAM Period, *P* 2, from *natural* behaviour occurring in the POS Period, *P* 3. The asterisk signifies that the variance due to subjects-within-groups is significant at $\alpha = 0.01$. As in Tables IV, VI, VII, VIII the comparison is within-subjects, and $n = 8$.

	Variable	F	DF	P less than
Cumulative duration	X LK	3.569	1.7	0.25
	X TK	1.117	1.7	
	X + Y LK	6.619	1.7	0.05 SIG
	X + Y TK	4.073	1.7	0.10
	X LK + TK	1.899	1.7	0.25
	X LK + Y TK	1.076	1.7	
Average duration	X LK	2.046	1.7	0.25
	X TK	0.147	1.7	
	X + Y LK	7.298	1.7	0.05 SIG
	X + Y TK	1.257	1.7	
	X LK + TK	0.014	1.7	
	X LK + Y TK	0.100	1.7	
Frequency min^{-1}	X LK	0.738	1.7	
	X TK	5.810	1.7	0.05 SIG
	X + Y LK	0.690	1.7	
	X + Y TK	91.830	1.7	0.01 SIG**
	X LK + TK	4.172	1.7	0.10
	X LK + Y TK	2.689	1.7	0.25

Here, the analysis was intended to discriminate between game playing and *natural* behaviour. Results of this repeated-measures analysis of variance for eight subjects are presented in Table IV.

The other possibility was that television, as the medium of interaction, influenced the behaviour of the participants. Consequently, a second analysis of variance compared *natural* conversation occurring via the video-telephone in *P* 2, with *natural* conversation occurring face-to-face, in *P* 3. The results of this analysis are presented in Table V.

Unfortunately, the participants never played the game face-to-face in the course of the experiment, so the influence of the medium upon game-playing could not be examined directly. However, a comparison of game-playing via video-telephone (*P* 2) with face-to-face conversation (*P* 3) was used in conjunction with the above analyses to ascertain whether the

TABLE VI

Results of univariate analysis of variance for each of six variables. In this case, the one-way analysis compares 'game' behaviour occurring in the GAM Period, *P* 2, with *natural* behaviour occurring in the POS Period, *P* 3. The asterisks signify that variance due to subjects-within-groups is significant at (*) $\alpha = 0.05$ or (**) $\alpha = 0.01$.

	Variable	F	DF	P less than
Cumulative duration	X LK	3.540	1.7	0.25
	X TK	0.843	1.7	
	X + Y LK	153.037	1.7	0.01 SIG**
	X + Y TK	3.843	1.7	0.10
	X LK + TK	14.654	1.7	0.01 SIG
	X LK + Y TK	2.752	1.7	0.25
Average duration	X LK	1.570	1.7	0.25
	X TK	43.829	1.7	0.01 SIG
	X + Y LK	3.670	1.7	0.10
	X + Y TK	0.291	1.7	
	X LK + TK	4.350	1.7	0.10
	X LK + Y TK	11.480	1.7	0.05 SIG
Frequency min^{-1}	X LK	1.082	1.7	
	X TK	7.402	1.7	0.05 SIG
	X + Y LK	8.707	1.7	0.05 SIG
	X + Y TK	16.541	1.7	0.01 SIG*
	X LK + TK	0.894	1.7	
	X LK + Y TK	0.549	1.7	

video-telephone was contributing to the difference between game-playing and *natural* conversation when both occurred via this medium. The results of this third analysis are presented in Table VI.

Note that all of the data for the three analyses summarised in Tables IV to VI were obtained from the same set of eight subjects; hence, all comparisons are within-subject. The group-means for each experimental

TABLE VII

Means for cumulative and average duration, and frequency. All means in (A), (B), and (C) were obtained from the 8 conversants used in the analysis presented in Tables IV, V, VI.

	Variable	Game (P 2)	Natural (P 2)	Natural (P 3)
Cumulative	X LK	28	67	48
duration	X TK	25	42	32
	X + Y LK	7	46	24
	X + Y TK	5	12	2
	X LK + TK	7	27	17
	X LK + Y TK	10	31	21

(A) Means for cumulative duration as a percentage of total time.

	Variable	Game (P 2)	Natural (P 2)	Natural (P 3)
Average	X LK	2.09	4.37	2.89
duration	X TK	1.39	2.31	2.55
	X + Y LK	0.95	2.24	1.29
	X + Y TK	0.51	0.78	0.45
	X LK + TK	0.74	1.46	1.40
	X LK + Y TK	0.95	1.69	1.57

(B) Means for average duration, in seconds.

	Variable	Game (P 2)	Natural (P 2)	Natural (P 3)
Frequency	X LK	8.05	8.54	10.12
	X TK	12.45	10.61	7.86
	X + Y LK	5.61	10.39	11.16
	X + Y TK	5.64	6.52	2.53
	X LK + TK	6.63	10.19	7.54
	X LK + Y TK	6.80	10.04	8.18

(C) Means for frequency per minute.

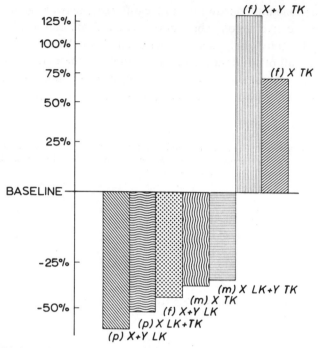

Fig. 5a.   Distinct changes is interpersonal events induced by the constraints of game-playing, as a percentage of the base level seen in face-to-face conversation. The peak (or nadir) of each deviation from the baseline is statistically significant.

(f) = frequency; (m) = mean length; (p) = proportion i.e. cumulative duration as a percentage of total time.

condition are shown in Table VII. These have been selectively arranged in Figures 5a to c in order to chart the changes in behaviour which were induced by the two factors (a) constraints imposed by the game-playing situation, and (b) mediation of interaction by the video-telephone. These changes have been graphed as a percentage of the 'base-level' which was observed in face-to-face conversation.

V. THE EFFECTS OF GAME-PLAYING ON
INTERPERSONAL BEHAVIOUR

The game-playing situation had profound effects on interaction. Although the amount of time spent in speaking was not greater than normal,

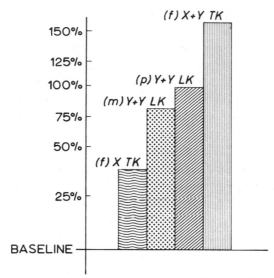

Fig. 5b. Distinct changes in interpersonal events induced by television as a medium of conversation, as a percentage of the base level seen in face-to-face conversation. The peak of each deviation from the baseline is statistically significant.

(f) = frequency; (m) = mean length; (p) = proportion, i.e. cumulative duration as a percentage of total time.

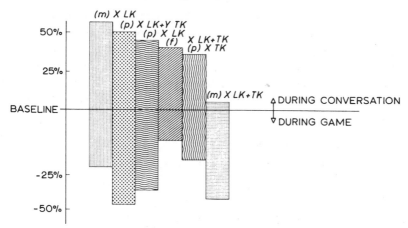

Fig. 5c. Differential changes in the same interpersonal events induced by television and by game-playing, as a percentage of the base level seen in face-to-face conversation. During conversation via video-telephone, television shifted behavior above the baseline; during game-playing, the constraints of the game had the opposite effect. Here, deviations from the baseline are not significant; however, the differences between peaks and nadirs are statistically significant for all six events.

(f) = frequency; (m) = mean length; (p) = proportion, i.e. cumulative duration as a percentage of total time.

the utterances became shorter and more frequent. This can be attributed to the nature of the game, which required the exchange of simple factual information, namely, where each player was moving (Figure 4). The point of interest here is that, with this change in verbal behaviour, there was a change in the use of glance. The proportion of looking might be expected to drop, since the game required the participants to look at their playing boards between moves, and the game was mildly competitive. However, this was not the case, for there was change, not in the amount of looking, but in the way that looking occurred. There was a smaller proportion of looking while talking, and the mean length of glance while listening was shorter. The sample in Figure 4 illustrates a trend seen throughout the game period: the speaker looked at the listener only near the end of his own utterance, then looked away shortly after the listener began to speak. When this pattern of looking prevails, mutual glance will be very infrequent. The data show that this was the case; although its mean length did not change, mutual glance became much less frequent, and occupied a smaller proportion of time during the game.

This suggests that, during the game, the pattern of looking was determined by the pattern of speaking, that very little visual interaction was occurring. Stapley (1972) has devised a simple formula for determining the amount of mutual glance to be expected if two conversants coordinate their glances with their speaking and listening behaviour. Briefly, the formula gives an estimate of the amount of mutual glance which is due to chance overlap of 'X looking while talking' and 'Y looking while listening'.

Expected mutual glance =

$$= \frac{(B_X)(A_Y)}{U_X} + \frac{(A_X)(B_Y)}{U_Y} + \frac{(L_X - A_X - B_X)(L_Y - A_Y - B_Y)}{T - U_X - U_Y}$$

where

U_X = total duration of utterance by X
U_Y = total duration of utterance by Y
A_X = total duration of 'X looks at and listens to Y'
A_Y = total duration of 'Y looks at and listens to X'
B_X = total duration of 'X looks at Y while talking'
B_Y = total duration of 'Y looks at X while talking'
L_X = total duration of 'X looks at Y'

L_Y = total duration of 'Y looks at X'
T = total duration of the interaction.

For each sample of conversation used in the comparison of 'game' with *natural* behaviour, a value for expected mutual glance was calculated. This value was subtracted from the value for mutual glance actually obtained in the respective conversations. The 'expected' and 'difference' scores were appropriately transformed to remove negative values and homogenise variance, then used as criterion measurements in analysis of variance. Again, all comparisons were within-subjects.

The fact that significantly different amounts of mutual glance were expected from 'game' and *natural* behaviour (Table VIII) reflects the difference in verbal behaviour between playing a game and conversing normally. The data shows that, in the case of conversation, this expectation was exceeded; whereas in the game, the much lower expectation was not met. In fact, it can be shown by applying the Wilcoxon matched-pair signed rank test (Siegel, 1956) to all the data for the game period that there was no real difference between the amount of mutual glance expected and the amount obtained. On the other hand, the data for *natural* conversation show, for the most part, real and positive differences (Table XI).

TABLE VIII

Results of univariate analysis of variance with 'game' versus *natural* behaviour as the lone factor. Both samples are drawn from the GAM Period, P 2. The comparison is within-subject, and $n = 4$.

Variable	F	DF	P less than
Expected mutual glance	13.227	1.3	0.05 SIG
Obtained minus expected	18.564	1.3	0.05 SIG

TABLE IX

Results of univariate analysis of variance comparing *natural* behaviour occurring in the GAM Period, P 2, with *natural* behaviour occurring in the POS Period, P 3. The comparison is within-subject, and $n = 4$.

Variable	F	DF	P less than
Expected mutual glance	2.626	1.3	
Obtained minus expected	0.023	1.3	

TABLE X

Means for cumulative duration as a percentage of total time, for the samples
used in the analysis of variance in Tables VIII and IX.

Variable	Game (P 2)	Natural (P 2)	Natural (P 3)
Expected mutual glance	10.7	45.2	24.0
Obtained minus expected	− 1.0	+ 0.8	+ 1.1

TABLE XI

Results of applying Wilcoxon's matched-pairs signed-rank
test to the differences between *expected* and *obtained* mutual
glance for all data. This test considers both the magnitude
and the direction of the differences. The mean differences
presented below are absolute values, for cumulative duration as per cent total time. Although the means for GAM
are the largest, they conceal the fact that nearly one-third
of the differences are negative.

		PRE	GAM	POS
Friends	N	9	11	11
	Mean diff.	2.3	3.3	3.1
	P less than	0.01 SIG		0.01 SIG
Strangers	N	6	11	10
	Mean diff.	1.9	2.4	2.2
	P less than	0.05 SIG		

In other words, the players in the game co-ordinated their glances at
one another with their speech, so that mutual glance was the result of
chance overlap of one player looking while speaking and the other player
looking while listening. This interpretation is also supported by a curious
result in Stapley (1972). Using the same video-telephone link and game,
Stapley examined changes in looking behaviour as the medium varied
from monochrome image, to cartoon image, to audio channel alone.[3]
Of course, in this last condition, the separated subjects could not see one
another; they continued to look at the blank screen. In this case there
was no visual feedback from glance; consequently, the amount and
average duration of looking dropped. However, the lack of this feedback

did not affect *looking synchrony*, for the amount of 'mutual glance' obtained was not significantly different from that expected if the subjects were co-ordinating their looking with their speech!

On the other hand, in normal conversation, there was significantly more mutual glance than could be accounted for by this mechanism. In normal conversation, there seemed to be a small but statistically significant amount of mutual glance which was due to visual rather than verbal interaction. This has been rigourously demonstrated for strangers, since the samples wherein both game and natural behaviour occurred adjacently happened to involve strangers. However, application of Wilcoxon's test to the differences obtained from friends indicates that, in this respect, they used glance in the same way as strangers (Table XI).

VI. THE EFFECT OF TELEVISION AS A MEDIUM OF INTERPERSONAL BEHAVIOUR

When television mediated interaction it had very complex effects on behaviour (Figure 5). Since mutual glance was partly determined by visual interaction in normal conversation (Table XI) an artificial visual medium such as television might be expected to increase this type of activity; and so it did. In fact, it increased all types of looking, at least marginally. For some reason it also increased the frequency of speech (and hence, joint utterance) during conversation. These increases in looking and speaking may both have been due to the fact that the video-telephone presented, almost immediately, a physically distant event, thereby intensifying both the awareness of the other, and the feeling of being watched. 'Curiosity' may have led to more looking, and social uneasiness to more speaking. In this regard, it should be noted that the video-telephone focused attention on the other person, since only a head and shoulders image of him was available. One effect of this was to eliminate nuance in the direction of gaze; the difference between looking at the other and looking away became very sharp.

Similar changes in behaviour have been attributed to the physical rather than social distance between the conversants. When the other person is viewed on a television screen, he appears to be at a greater distance than the size of the retinal image warrants (Stapley, 1972). As the distance between two conversants increases, the amount of mutual glance which is related to both speaking and listening increases (Stephenson *et al.*, 1972). Conceivably, the video-telephone used in the present experiment influenced the conversants to behave as if they were more distant than in the face-to-face situation.

Similarly, the effect of television was to increase looking, speaking, and also looking both while speaking and while listening, although the higher levels were not statistically different from those seen in face-to-face conversation. But this was the case only when television mediated *natural* conversation, for the medium interacted in an interesting way with the type of exchange. This interaction is charted in Figure 5(c): during conversation, television exerted its typical influence on interpersonal behaviour; however, when the type of social intercourse changed, the constraints of the game gained ascendancy over the effects of the medium of exchange. So, in normal conversation, the apparent distance between the conversants was probably salient in shifting behaviour in one direction, whereas, in the game, the pattern of verbal interaction shifted behaviour towards the opposite pole.

VII. SUMMARY

In this study, statistically real differences in interactive behaviour have been induced in the laboratory. This has been accomplished by selective matching of conversants and by manipulation of the conditions under which they met. Apparently, these conditions can be manipulated in such a way as to induce *natural* conversation, for the transcripts showed that the conversants relaxed completely over long periods, broached intimate areas of discourse, and behaved in a manner suggesting that they did not feel themselves observed. Furthermore, the differences in speech and glance seemed to vindicate the distinction made between game-playing and *natural* conversation – between behaviour motived extrinsically and behaviour motivated intrinsically.

In a limited sample of male university undergraduates, the imposition of goals and rules of conduct (as in the game period) significantly decreased the use of glance, apparently by shifting verbal interaction to a pattern which restricted the frequency and length of glance.

Mediation of interaction by television had generally opposite effects on the use of glance, probably by convincing the conversants that they were physically more distant from one another than they would have been in face-to-face conversation.

The main intention in this project has been development and demonstration of experimental techniques for the meaningful study of social interaction. The results show that use of a game to simulate 'interaction' can produce misleading data. This suggests that a closer analysis of the relation between the 'goals' and 'rules' of the simulation and the thing simulated should precede experimentation. For instance, the constraints on behaviour operative in an interview situation may be parallel to those operative in a game of the Deutsch-Krause type. Analysis of this sort might well produce a classification of different types of social interaction.

The project demonstrated that samples of every-day conversation can be collected experimentally and that relevant factors can be manipulated in a 'natural experiment'. A large set of interpersonal events has served as useful data. This set lends itself to real measurement, but other types are also practical. For instance, the recorded transcript proved necessary to make the distinction between game and normal conversation (Figure 4). Content analysis of sample transcripts revealed the conversants' lexical styles (in the fashion of Schegloff, 1971). In one case, a conversant's repeated use of the phrase 'you know' was explored by relating each usage to the speaker's concomitant use of glance.

Although the impact of degree of acquaintance (factor F) upon looking, speaking, etc. seemed small, its impact upon pause length was significant. Strangers paused for statistically shorter times than friends, regardless of whether they were playing the game or conversing freely. Friends lengthened their pauses as they moved from game to conversation (compare Jaffe and Feldstein, 1970).

Finally, some of the 'compatibility' measures obtainable through the FIRO-B questionnaire proved useful indicators of shared glance. As predictive measures, they may be more promising than the raw FIRO scores (compare Excline et al., 1965).

Taken together, the results of the project encourage further experimental study of everyday social interaction. Our personal knowledge of social events is very rich, yet our scientific knowledge of them is scant. Science has unfolded the rare and esoteric, but has only begun to offer explanation of our most common experiences of life.

50   DENNIS DICKS

ACKNOWLEDGEMENT

The author wishes to thank Professor Colin Cherry, the Canada Council, and many colleagues for their intellectual, financial, and technical support during this project.

Department of Electrical Engineering,
Queen's University Kingston, Ontario, Canada

NOTES

[1] *Dyad* here means a pair of people conversing.
[2] See under Deutsch and Krause (1961) in Bibliography.
[3] Cartoon images were produced by electronically processing television pictures, using 'edge detectors', resulting in a type of line drawing image, resembling hand drawn cartoons.

BIBLIOGRAPHY

Birdwhistell, R. L., 'Kinesics and Communication', in *Explorations in Communication* (ed. by E. Carpenter and M. McLuhan), Beacon, Boston, 1960, pp. 54–64.
Deutsch, M. and Krause, R. M., 'The Effect of Threat on Interpersonal Bargaining', *J. Abnorm. Soc. Psychol.* 63 (1961) 181–189.
Exline, R. V., Gray, D., and Schuette, D., 'Visual Behaviour in a Dyad as Affected by Interview Content, and Sex of Respondent', *J. Pers. Soc. Psychol.* 1 (1965) 201–209.
Jaffe, J. and Feldstein, S., *Rhythms of Dialogue*, Academic Press, N.Y., 1970.
Kendon, A. and Cook, M., 'The Consistency of Gaze-Patterns in Social Interaction', *Br. J. Psychol.* 60 (1969) 481–494.
Krause, F., 'An Investigation of Verbal Exchanges between Strangers', *Dissert. Abs. Intl.*, Univ. of Michigan, Ref. 30-3-1235A, 1969.
Schegloff, E. A., 'Notes on Conversational Practice: Formulating Place', *Language and Social Context* (ed. by P. P. Giglioli), Penguin, London, 1971.
Schutz, W. C., 'The FIRO Scales Manual', *Consulting Psychologist's Press*, Palo Alto, California, 1967.
Siegel, E., *Non-Parametric Statistics for the Behavioural Sciences*, McGraw-Hill, N.Y. 1956.
Sommer, R., 'Studies in Personal Space', *Sociometry* 22 (1959) 247–260.
Stapley, B., 'Visual Enhancement of Telephone Conversations', Doctoral thesis, Imperial College, University of London, 1972.
Stephenson, G. M., Rutter, D. R., and Dore, S., 'Eye-Contact, Distance, and Affiliation', Paper presented at Oxford Workshop on Gaze, Oxford, March 1972.

AARON V. CICOUREL

INTERVIEWING AND MEMORY*

This paper examines information processing problems associated with decisions made during medical history interviewing, and links these decisions to the use of questionnaires with fixed-choice responses. In a medical history interview the physician's summary statement does not reveal the reasoning employed in posing questions and deciding that appropriate answers have been obtained. The use of self-contained stimulus questions with fixed response choices in sample surveys poses a similar problem. In survey research we need to clarify the reasoning attributed to the respondent, and the researcher's decision-making, in arriving at acceptable questions, answers and relationships among stipulated variables. These two strategies for obtaining information do not deal adequately with the emergent conditions of interview settings. The emergent conditions include spontaneous variations in the language used, several levels of semantic information processing, shifting definitions of the problem and a problematic use of stimulus questions. These conditions, seen as natural to all interviewing, will be addressed in this paper.

I. THE SURVEY RESEARCH MODEL

The decision model used by researchers employing fixed-choice interviews for collecting a data base seeks to correlate the respondent's everyday experiences with independent variables like age, sex, religion, education, and occupation. These variables are said to contribute to the respondent's responses because they organize his recognition of and orientation to his environment. In this survey research model the researcher's theory specifies how the respondent's past experiences and structural characteristics provide for choices from among a specifiable set of alternatives available. The respondent's selections, therefore, are assumed to reflect an internalized value system that is activated by the different consequences attributed to each of the alternatives. Variations in the perception of alternatives and their consequences provide the

C. Cherry (ed.), Pragmatic Aspects of Human Communication, 51–82. All Rights Reserved
Copyright © 1974 by D. Reidel Publishing Company, Dordrecht-Holland

survey researcher with information about the respondent's values or attitudes and an understanding of group norms. Structural variables of age, sex, parental occupations, education, residence, religion, are said to 'locate' the respondent in the 'social structures.' The variables provide the researcher with a data base for the construction of social indicators to depict the respondent's childhood and adult experiences and orientations to his or her environment.

Two important methodological consequences follow from the survey researcher's use of interviewing. (1) Questionnaires can be used to ask subjects about values and attitudes as expressed in fixed-choice elicitation procedures. (2) Behavioral consequences of the attitudes or values registered by the questionnaire can be imputed to respondents and correlated with structural variables. These correlations can then be linked to characteristics found in the general population as depicted in census and vital-statistics data.

Although the interviewing-questionnaire research strategy presumes a deductive specification of respondent responses and their clustering according to the theoretical assumptions that motivated the questions, few surveys may achieve this ideal. In actual practice new questions, and questions that 'worked' in past studies are used. The questionnaire items that produce significant differences are then linked to theoretical issues, but often in an *ad hoc* manner. The pre-testing of questionnaire items seldom means a restructuring of the general theory, but merely the restatement of a few general hypotheses. Explicit hypotheses are formulated usually after the marginal tabulations have been obtained. An extensive search procedure is employed to generate possibly significant relationships based on the cross-tabulation of different questionnaire items. The persistent discrepancy between the planning of surveys, and their continual *post hoc* analysis, despite ambiguous replications, is seldom attributable to an impoverished theoretical basis for understanding the processing and representation of information in interviews.

Traditional uses of interviewing in social science assume that the problems of obtaining information from respondents can be minimized or eliminated by careful training of interviewers. The standardization of questions and pre-testing of questionnaire items are also cited as safeguards against the idiosyncracies of the interview. Deciding what is an 'appropriate' question and a meaningful 'answer' to the question is anticipated by the use of standardized questions carefully examined during and after pre-tests.

The traditional view of interviewing provides for a logic of questions and answers that standardizes the output or response categories so that cross-tabulations are readily produced. The format is seen as an obvious way to elicit stored information. How stored information is organized and how access is to be made is not defined as a serious problem. The researcher assumes the respondent will be presented with 'normal' speaking intonation, standardized syntactic structures, and standardized topics as indexed by the same lexical items. Open-ended questions that encourage spontaneous responses are not encouraged because this complicates the coding of responses and the achievement of a standardized format.

The organization of stored experiences, however, may require different formats and subroutines for their elicitation. The respondent's monitoring of his or her own output and the interviewer's reactions, provides a feedback that can trigger off other items of stored information that a standardized fixed-choice question can block. Participants usually begin an interview with vague conceptions of what is going to happen. They begin to assume common meanings that emerge implicitly and explicitly over the course of the interview. These emergent meanings provide an implicit working background that can help clarify the participants' questions and answers. This negotiated clarification process occurs in all interviewing, including the pre-tests that are part of creating fixed-choice questionnaires. But these negotiated exchanges do not become part of the data base used for making inferences reflected in the medical history summary or survey findings.

The standardized survey questionnaire does not include in its data base interpretations made by participants during the pre-tests or final interview. The standardization of the questionnaire format forces the respondent to find 'appropriateness' in what is offered by the interviewer. Standardization of questions and answers masks how a question triggers off pre-processing and a memory search procedure to decide that the question is appropriate, unclear, not relevant to past experiences, requires further explanation, or is so foolish or annoying that a misleading response is provided.

The use of fixed-choice questionnaires is expedient for obtaining huge amounts of information from a sizable sample said to be representative of a larger population. The social scientist sacrifies validity for reliability by seeking information that is amenable to tabular form. The survey format ignores the progressive elaboration of meanings in the encounter. The fixed-choice questionnaire seeks to eliminate the self-conscious accounting that normally takes place after an attempt by one party to elicit information from another person. The fixed-choice format detaches the questions and answers from the original conditions of interaction or experience being addressed, and also divorces the interview setting from how the memory search provides the context within which questions will be understood and answers produced.

The social science survey has formalized some aspects of common linguistic interrogative techniques normally learned by members of some group. The formalization, however, did not emerge after a careful exam-ination of how members of a group normally use interrogative procedures. There have been attempts to link the interview to cognitive studies of how persons process information during all social exchanges (Hyman *et al.*, 1954). But the questionnaire responses are presumed to 'speak for them-selves' in the form of tabulated printouts that summarize a sample's attitudes and general knowledge about themselves, objects, events, and others.

The question-answer format is presented as an 'objective' algorithm. This algorithm's success depends on the researcher's careful pre-testing of questions and training of interviewers to find 'appropriate' information possessed by the respondent. The survey research strategy is a weak approach to the elicitation of information from respondents because it contrasts with recent work on information processing, discussed below.

II. MEMORY AND THE ANSWERING OF QUESTIONS

The study of types of questions that are important in natural languages, where a formal grammar exists, can provide a rough ideal logic of ques-tions of the form where the questioner (Harrah, 1973):

(a)   Is presumed to know what the problem is about.
(b)   Knows how to express the question in an effective manner.
(c)   Knows what the set of possible alternatives can be.

(d)   Can claim that one of the alternatives is true.
(e)   Does not know which alternative he wants to know.
(f)   Believes the respondent can help him if a particular question
         is put properly.

There are various logics of questions (Harrah, 1973) and they can involve different conditions such as a classroom setting where a teacher puts questions to students and knows the answers expected of students. Or the situation can be a Ph.D. examination (described by Harrah) where the questions put by the examining committee may be designed to help the student or irritate or confuse or attack each other and not the student. The situation can be one where many questions are put to search for a general pattern that would suggest an underlying problem. In the medical field a central nervous system disorder can produce symptoms that may over-lap significantly with a serious form of food poisoning or temporary head injury. Hence the sequential order of the questions and answers may not be relevant. In some situations it may be important to match each reply with the question to which it is a reply. Other possibilities include asking another question in response to a question until the questioner is made to clarify his presumed original intention.

In the case of questioning in social-behavioral studies the object is to generate a reply for each preceding question. In the medical interview the questions can come in clusters, to see if a pattern emerges that can be related to several theories about the central nervous system functioning, endocrine balance, enzyme deficiencies, etc. But in all of these cases, including those described by Harrah in his review of the literature, the assumption made is that the conditions of information processing can be held constant or that they are irrelevant to the ideal or standard conditions employed. The model of questioning does not specify the constraints of information processing upon both participants and observer or analyst within or across the use of different sensory modalities.

A recent paper by Norman (in press) suggests several relationships between memory and the answering of questions. He notes that the question may be phrased differently from the storage format needed for retrieving the necessary information (called the 'paraphrase problem'). The 'best' answer to a question may prove to be a question by the respondent to pinpoint what is intended by the original question. Norman is concerned with the pre-processing that occurs before an answer to a question is provided. Hence we need to know something about how people store information, how they combine general information they possess and link it to what is addressed by the question. The reasons or explanations that respondents add to their answers provides some clues about how the question was understood.

Of general interest here is the fact that no simple algorithm can be identified that would specify a sequence of instructions or steps or actions leading to a direct question-answer solution (Norman, in press). Norman suggests that the retrieval process is a construction by the respondent because of the paraphrase problem. Short-term memory limitations may influence the retrieval process indirectly because respondents may not be able to parse instructions or questions that are too long and complicated.

The question-answer interview situation can be influenced by such factors as syntactic information, general knowledge of people and of the world, the format in which original experiences are stored, selective attention and memory limitations at the time of receiving the question, dialect differences, and non-verbal information. This list should also include the participants' reflexive monitoring of their own activities, and the emergent and changing atmosphere of the setting. Oral or written representations of the questions and answers invariably require elaboration by the participants to be understood (Cicourel, in press [a]). Hence a model of the representation of information in memory presumes there is an expansion of the underlying meanings of actions and concepts (Norman, in press). We should not submit open-ended answers immediately to a data reduction process, as is usually the case in social science survey research. But what can we say about questions designed to limit possible responses to a few choices? Presumably the questions have been carefully designed and pre-tested with preliminary samples of respondents to insure their meaningfulness. The use of questions that require fixed-choice responses ignores the information processing problems inherent in all social exchanges. The questions are assumed to be the 'right' questions and properly limited in the choices they provide. Researchers justify the use of this format by the fact that respondents are willing to submit to such procedures.

The logic of questions described by Harrah (1973) does not make problematic the questioner's ability to encode his thoughts or intentions into language that will be understood by the respondent. Nor is adequate attention paid to the respondent's ability to parse or decode the message, and to link the information so derived to his own knowledge. Similarly, the questioner cannot be assumed to possess an infallible ability to decode the respondent's responses. A basic problem is to decide how much and what types of information we can receive and generate, given the limitations of processing many items of information, and where each item is limited by the number of elements it may contain (Miller, 1956). The kinds of syntactic structures used may place constraints on what information can be processed if the utterances used are long and contain embedded relative clauses that require extra effort to link agent to action to object. The contingencies of information processing are like a moving target. The 'parsers' and emergent meanings used by the questioner and respondent cannot be assumed to be passive aspects of how each will understand the questions and answers.

The physician is often unclear about the patient's medical problems when he enters his interview with the patient. He will often begin to hypothesize about possible alternatives almost immediately. Each hypothesis can trigger off one or more subroutines requiring information retrieval from his own and the patient's memory, thus leading to question-answer sequences that change their course and content sometimes abruptly. The physician obviously believes the patient can help him if different questions are put properly. But considerable negotiation may be required in moving back and forth between the ideas inherent in the physician's questions, and the patient's ability to connect the questions to his own experiences.

The physician's knowledge of medicine will vary depending on the kinds of cases he handles frequently and his possible speciality. A useful analogy exists in chess. The expert or master chess player is able to recognize different 'good' and 'bad' moves more easily than the weak player. There are striking differences in how the expert or the weak player can reconstruct a chess position after only five seconds of exposure to the board (Simon and Barenfeld, 1969; Chase and Simon, 1973). The physician familar with some speciality will learn to ask questions that index his experiences with certain classes of patients. When the specialist asks questions and receives answers from a patient the reasoning he uses is seldom revealed in a medical history report. Hence not all physicians using the report would be able to reconstruct the specialist's decision-making strategies in formulating 'appropriate' questions and deciding on 'appropriate' answers.

One way to examine the issues described thus far is to contrast a medical summary and the tape-recorded interview materials generated by an internal medical specialist and his patient. The medical history summary statement suffers from the same problems raised earlier on survey questionnaires. The data bases of each are idealized summary statements that mask the constructed character or reasoning which produces information labelled 'findings.' In the example chosen here the medical history summary statement which I discuss below was dictated by the physician immediately after the interview and was based on his brief written notes and memory of the exchange. (See Appendix I)

III. ANSWERING QUESTIONS IN A MEDICAL INTERVIEW

The medical summary statement begins with a brief description of the patient's problem of high blood pressure and when it was first noticed. (See Appendix IIA, *The Initial Statement of the Medical History Summary*.) But before we examine the medical history summary, I shall discuss how the physician actually interviewed the patient about her problem.

After the preliminaries of acknowledging the tape-recording of the interview and resolving the fact that the patient did not completely fill out the questionnaire (7–10 in Appendix I), the Interviewer asks (13) *Now just tell me your (slight pause) primary (slight pause) problem that you want us to focus on. What is bothering you at the moment?* The patient's response in (14) refers to the 'primary problem' of what her previous doctor told her, and suggests she is at the office of Dr. X because of the other physician's referral. A variety of terms have been used and assumed by both parties to be 'clear'. Hence in (14) when the patient says: *Well, Dr. B said I had high blood pressure*, the patient is not providing physical symptoms for the interviewer, but seems to be establishing the grounds for the present interview. The patient seems to have ignored the interviewer's remark of *What is bothering you at the moment?*

I assumed that the information contained in (1) through (12) and the first part of (13) is accompanied by the perception of normal appearences and talk that each can treat as unremarkable. I arbitrarily decided to view the first part of the interview as unremarkable and ignore its content, assuming that the first serious topic for the interviewer began in (13). Notice that this means viewing (1) and (2) as normal greetings and not a serious attempt on the part of the physician to make inquiries into the patient's general health. I knew that the interview took place in the doctor's office and the patient was ostensibly there for medical reasons. I ignored the opening lines of the interview to focus on the contrast between the medical history summary and the details of the interview the summary presumably reflects.

The remarks in (7) on the medical history form implies that each was anticipating the other's remarks and filling in details for the other. The interviewer says *Good (slight pause) great*, in response to (6), and then topicalizes the problem of the history form. He is interrupted by the patient. Neither the patient nor the interviewer demanded an elaboration of the other's remarks, nor did either question the other about their respective actions. The patient's *I haven't* could mean 'I haven't filled it out,' or 'I haven't finished it', etc. The interviewer could have been examining the history form and decided she meant the form was not completed, but that it had been filled out partially. The interviewer's continued remarks *That's alright, I'll go through it with you* implies that he will cover the same ground during his interview and elicit the missing information. The patient's remarks in (10) reveal a general problem of spontaneous oral exchanges. The interviewer and researcher must supply missing details to provide coherence to the remarks by linking it to what is said in (7) and (8). The dialogue seems to follow a neat QAQAQA sequencing order, because our method of representation gives that impression.

Trying to represent the dialogue as I think I heard it after five, ten, and fifteen replays of the recorder is difficult. I am constrained by the sequential ordering that is a built-in feature of our way of writing. If we seek to use a linguistic model constrained by ideal-normative model sentences with an SVO construction, we would have to create grammatical sentences or face serious obstacles to an analysis. My analysis is influenced by the way I transcribe the tape and by tacit reliance on my native competence as a speaker-hearer. There is the additional problem: my careful listening alerts me to details that the participants may have ignored as irrelevant. But then I could ignore details the participants viewed as basic to their understanding of the exchange. Various aspects of their speech habits are a normal part of their repertoire and may not be designed to communicate anything special in the present setting. The researcher invariably exaggerates the significance of the dialogue by the way he or she represents its content in some organized sequential form, and by the way he or she focuses on particular features of the dialogue.

The interview took place during the first scheduled appointment between the patient and Dr. X. There is no reason to believe that this particular case is not typical of medical interviews. The interview begins (see Appendix I) with an explanation of why the exchange is being tape-recorded. A discussion of the 'immediate problem' follows where it was noted that the patient's blood pressure was found to be elevated during a second pregnancy. The interviewer asks about other symptoms that might be associated with the high blood pressure (21). A discussion of headaches (25) follows. Then the patient mentions her dislike of physicians. There is an attempt to link the headaches with other symptoms, especially visual problems (21–48).

The initial statement of the medical history summary on the 'immediate problem' (Appendix IIA) emerged after about eleven minutes into the interview. There is a discrepancy between the initial paragraph the physician describes as the 'immediate problem' and the actual interview dialogue. Appendix IIA and B reveal how information is condensed into a form that is medically clear but ambiguous as to how the physician reasoned in creating the condensed summary statement. The same problems occur when non-medical interviews are summarized. The first sentence of the summary (Appendix IIA) is *The patient was first told of modest blood pressure elevation at age 31 when she consulted an American physician in Japan for palpitations and chest discomfort.* This observation summarizes the dialogue from (93) to (103). The interviewer (93) asks the patient to delay discussing her present blood pressure condition while he inquires into her past history of blood pressure elevation. Her remarks (94–98) casually refer to *that fellow in Japan.* There is a confusion here about the identity of *that fellow in Japan.* I return to this point below.

The interviewer establishes the patient's age indirectly (101–103) by asking when the examination in Japan occurred. Her present age was established earlier in (33) (see Appendix I). The interviewer expresses surprise (103) at the patient's visit to a doctor because of earlier remarks (40–43) that she didn't like the medical profession and avoided seeing physicians. He infers that the patient *must have had a complaint then*. The patient describes her problem as ... *I was having pains in, and uh, and you know my heart you know (slight pause) was acting funny....* The interviewer's remarks (105) refers to *Your heart beating fast and you had some chest discomfort*, and this seems to be the basis for the summary statement.

The summary statement makes reference to an 'apparent' relation between the *palpitations* and *emotional stress*. But there is no follow-up in the interview at this time to suggest how the general home situation or patient's emotional status in Japan might have produced the symptoms. The summary statement's references to emotional stress probably stems from several general discussions in later parts of the exchange. Other parts of the summary statement provide brief remarks about the patient's father's hypertension, her family's frequent moves while a child and adolescent, and her frequent moves after marriage to a naval officer. There are additional remarks about a *severe depression* and psychiatric consultations associated with the first pregnancy. All of this information was provided in somewhat fragmented exchanges later in the interview with few details about the nature of the depression.

The reference to *palpitations* being related to *emotional stress* indicates how an interviewer taking a few notes would condense information from several independent items of an exchange to establish an account or explanation of symptoms. Another physician would not know the basis for the observation about the palpitations in Japan.

The reference to a negative EKG is discussed in (106-109) with the patient saying ... *they did one of those, those, things*. The interviewer supplied the term *electrocardiograms*. He then asked ... *what did the doctor say?* (107) and received the reply *He said it looked alright* (108). The patient's *he said it looked alright* is interpreted as a negative EKG (*it looked okay*) (109) in the summary statement.

The reference to phenobarbital in the summary statement is expressed in (108) where it is suggested that the patient was actually seen by two or three physicians. This takes us back to the examination in Japan when the patient said that she could not remember the name of the first physician she was referred to (94–97) (*who was that fellow in Japan?*), the Sunday her husband took her to the hospital. The patient continues to 'code' her experiences in Japan by indicating how she went in for another examination the next day (110) where *everything looked fine. And then I*

went in ...finally decided I'd better have... and Dr. G. said it was up a little.
The blood pressure was found to be elevated again. The reference to the
blood pressure being up a little in the summary statement does not reference the fact that the patient returned for a second and perhaps third
visit. The patient must have said 'blood pressure' in (110) for the interviewer (111) also said *...Dr. G. he found it to be up a bit.* The patient's *no*
here in (111) presumably was a response to the interviewer's reference to
the patient having seen one physician twice and having the blood pressure
taken *once, twice.* The patient's remarks in (110) could be interpreted as
her having seen one physician on the initial Sunday. Then she was *told to
come back the next day and see somebody else.* Her remarks *everything
looked fine, so I sad great forget it* could imply a second visit. The remark
then I went in ...finally decided I'd better have... could have been a third
visit when *Dr. G. said it was up a little bit.* The patient seems to clarify the
situation in (112) yet the number of visits is not clear nor the circumstances
under which the blood pressure was taken. My listening to the tape suggests that the interviewer experienced difficulty (as I did) trying to disen-
tangle the patient's remarks. The problem is not resolved in the following
comments (112) because after stressing the conditions for seeing physicians
in the military (112 *et seq*) the interviewer shifts the questioning to the first
pregnancy and hence leaves the issue unclarified.

The above interview sequences reveal several problems of selective
attention and how the contingencies of the exchange influence an interviewer's ability to clarify problems, and record and recall them for a
summary statement. The discrepancy between the summary statement
and the transcript of the tape-recorded interview reveal that alternate
interpretations of fact in the transcript are possible because of confusions
in the questioning and frequent use of retrospective formulations. A
central problem is how to decide we have obtained accurate information
when the interviewing conditions compound the question-answer format.
The patient cannot remember details, or she misleads the interviewer in
her description. The interviewer can't remember, after each answer,
whether he has obtained all the necessary details to establish a clear
sequence of events. No interview strategies were attempted that would
ask questions according to how the original experiences were stored.
The interviewer did not ask the patient to reconstruct the circumstances
of the visit in Japan three years earlier by first asking for the season

(summer, fall, winter, spring) to establish the date more accurately. Nor was the patient asked to describe her activities the day before and during the Sunday she asked her husband to take her to the physician. The possible family conditions or personal emotional experiences prior to and on the day of the visit to the physician are not explored. The idea of emotional stress might have been established immediately by the interviewer. Or perhaps the later information about a severe depression in 1964–1965 after the birth of the first child was retrospectively seen as the background for the high blood pressure in Japan in 1969.

At the time of the initial questioning on the high blood pressure there was no hint of a post-partum depression. The information (93–94) on the elevated blood pressure generated antecedent conditions for probing several possible sources of the elevation.

The opening paragraph in the further summary (Appendix IIIA) begins with a remark that modest elevation of *blood pressure during the third trimester of her second pregnancy* occurred. In Appendix IIIB the transcript reveals how the information was obtained. The interviewer in (13) asks for information on the *primary problem* and receives a response (14) indicating high blood pressure. The sequence (15–20) provides information that would establish the high blood pressure in the third trimester (*two and a half months before* the June delivery date).

The second sentence of the opening paragraph of the further summary statement (Appendix IIIA) reports a date of *about April 22nd* as the time when *the patient experienced intermittent episodes of visual disturbance characterized as 'dust' appearing in her visual field*. The transcript (21–24 in Appendix IIIC) establishes the appearance of *dust* in the visual field, but in (24) the patient reveals she should be wearing glasses but avoids wearing them *because I have a small nose and they're down here constantly*. When the interviewer (21) asks about symptoms associated with the high blood pressure at the time of her second pregnancy, the patient mentions the appearance of *dust*. The patient volunteers information about her wearing glasses. The interviewer may have reasoned that the high blood pressure but not the problem of not wearing her glasses would be linked to the appearance of *dust*. Then in (25) he asks about *headaches, for example*. This could be seen as a continuation of (21) and (23), or as an attempt to link her headaches to her not wearing the glasses. Here we have to know how the interviewer's knowledge of clinical medicine may have ruled out several hypotheses and confirmed others. The interviewer does not have an indefinite amount of time and may have reasoned that the remark about not wearing glasses is not significant unless there are persistent headaches. Such uncovering of a history of hypertension and a postpartum depression later in the interview may have convinced the interviewer retrospectively that the glasses not being worn was not a central problem.

The question about headaches (25) seems to be a follow-up of the patient's reporting not wearing her glasses, but this connection seems to be dropped after the patient refers to having a *tension headache right now*. The further summary statement (Appendix IIIA) contains a few remarks in a separate paragraph on this problem. The patient defines her headaches as a *tension headache* in the transcript (26) and as appearing *when I menstruate or just before my period* (32). The summary statement refers to the headaches as being *related to tension and also the onset of her menses*. The remarks in the medical history summary reflect a condensed and organized version of the transcript details (31–40). The details do not reveal the negotiation (35–40) between interviewer and patient on the frequency of the headaches. The headaches are not related to the non-wearing of glasses, but there is an attempt to explore the possibility of migraine conditions when the interviewer asks (43) about the headaches being associated with getting *sick to your stomach?* The interviewer's notes may heve reflected (26) and (32), thus linking the headaches to the hypertension. The patient tries to dismiss the headaches (34) and this may have influenced the interviewer's interpretation of them as, in part, due to her not wearing glasses. Yet in (43) the interviewer asks if the headaches are associated with seeing *double or do you have blurring of vision?*

When we contrast the summary statement with the transcript we are making a second guess at the way the interviewer may have pursued unstated hypotheses about the patient's problems and what might be associated with her referral 'for evaluation of hypertension'. My second-guessing reveals how the researcher's limitations are similar to those of the interviewer's. The researcher and interviewer are constrained by similar cognitive and linguistic or conversational elements in their construction of accounts of 'what happened'. What is important are the shifts in questioning contained in the transcript and the glosses in the summary statement that make clear ways in which the interviewer processed information during and immediately after the interview. The summary statement reveals specific interpretations that do not reflect the equivocalities of the transcript. But the summary does show how data reduction after the fact can produce appropriate medical categories. The categories permit the physician to prescribe a course of treatment and also becomes part of a medical record to facilitate decision-making by other physicians. The summary is also a legal document that indexes the application of medical knowledge, but does not permit a reconstruction of the contingencies of the interview.

The interviewer's knowledge of different topics (in this case medicine), and understanding of the patient's talk, creates evidence for deciding what to infer from various answers, and when enough information has been obtained to stop one line of questioning and to shift to a new topic.

The medical interviewer followed an implicit outline based on his experience with patients presenting themselves with 'high blood pressure'. His interviewing includes tacit observations of the patient's affect, physical appearance, movement, and use of language. There is a simultaneous concern with formulating questions that would elicit various types of information about the reason for referral. Meanwhile, as new information is received, details are being processed to generate possible new questions that would clarify problems already discussed. As information is received and processed, present details are related to prior particulars, or are recognized as having possible significance for an independent line of questioning.

The inferences that are made in the course of the interview must link present information to aspects of one's memory. The earlier details may be subjected to further elaboration depending on what follows. This abductive reasoning (Peirce, 1957), retrospectively linking consequent conditions to antecendent information, is a basic feature of all socially organized communication. Depending on the answers to some questions, others emerge as relevant, and the interviewer or respondent must assess the significance of information while continually asking further questions that may be related to an over-all pattern. The interviewer's (correspondent's) thinking about the significance of past answers can lead to questions about unstated hypotheses formulated during the interview.

Our ability, as interviewer or respondent, to comprehend two simultaneous messages can be attentuated if we divide our attention equally between the messages. Attending to several informational modalities and trying to sustain a dialogue that satisfies what we think of as 'normal discourse' means a steady flow of speech acts that do not contain 'long' pauses, 'frequent' hesitations, and incoherent use of lexical items. It is difficult to simulate this idea of 'normal discourse', by presenting a written transcript, but a few minutes of an audio tape can be quite convincing that someone's speech is 'bizarre'.

Several levels of information processing occur in an interview. These levels require us to shift back and forth between different informational sources while we link selected particulars to retrieved information in long-term memory. We may shift our attention from the patient's appearance or movement or voice intonation, to the content of what is being said. Or, we may note the possible significance of what is being presented by contrasting the information with prior details or some vague or general idea of an immediate or underlying problem. These numerous and continuous shifts in attention interact with our memory but may be recorded only minimally in the form of cryptic notes. Our notes can provide us with truncated descriptions designed to capture significant details, or with analytic remarks that mask the details we paid attention to.

The medical interview clarifies uses of interviews and questionnaires in social-behavioral science. The medical interviewer must negotiate a difficult interface between basic (and clinical) science concepts and vocabularies and common sense conceptions and terms dealing with illness and biological causality. The medical interviewer cannot 'pre-test' nor standardize his questions. The most experienced medical interviewer cannot escape the contingencies associated with a broad range of patients from different cultural backgrounds. The medical interviewer is seldom trained to deal with the contrast between the questions used and the common sense reasoning and language employed by both physician and patient. The emergent problems associated with linking medical-biological and common sense theoretical perspectives on health and pathology provide a natural laboratory for understanding the information processing parameters of everyday decision-making.

The structured interview or fixed-choice questionnaire attempts to minimize the information-processing difficulties associated with medical interviews. The attempt to minimize the difficulties of such face-to-face exchanges provides findings that are said to be 'objective'. But the structured interview or questionnaire achieves its 'objectivity' by employing an ambiguous model of language use and information processing. This model legislates the interface between questions and the respondent's responses instead of exposing the interface to careful study.

IV. THEORETICAL DISCUSSION

Non-verbal communication will not be considered in this paper. The data base consists of a tape-recorded interview and this was felt to be inadequate for a discussion of non-verbal activities (Cicourel, in press [b]). In our use of the interview we often forget that we can attend simultaneously to multiple sources of information that can be processed selectively at different levels of analysis. We usually represent our thoughts, feelings, and intentions through a verbal mode of communication that cannot recover the complexity of our experiences nor the complexity of the setting. To clarify the complex interaction that occurs in interviews we must understand something about how verbal communication filters different experiences.

The linguist views language as bounded utterances whose internal structure can be described by clearly identifiable rules. He refers to syntactic and phonological rules, and to the idea of a lexicon. In the lexicon each item or entry possesses a phonological matrix as well as inherent and contextual features that can specify the item as animate or abstract, and, for example, whether it follows a definite or indefinite article. This model provides the linguist with carefully constructed ideals that can be studied and described independently of actual language use in social settings.

The linguist's syntax-based theory of language provides the ideal structures needed to construct standardized questionnaires. The linguist's normative theory of language describes prescriptive and proscriptive rules or practices. Such practices are like recipes for deciding what is socially acceptable and unacceptable behavior. The language of the medical history summary and survey questions achieve their limited objectivity by relying on idealized language structures. The linguist's idealized grammatical and phonological rules, and standardized dictionary, however, are not helpful in the study of actual language use in interview settings, i.e., specific utterances.

An understanding of decision-making activities in interviews requires that we look beyond the linguist's model. Research on the interview as an information processing activity suggests that the human organism processes information using both a 'filter model' and something like analysis-by-synthesis (Broadbent, 1958; Neisser, 1967; Norman, 1969). The filter model seeks to explain the limitations of our ability to perceive competing messages by reference to perceptual factors. The brain is seen as capable of filter operations that are oriented to accepting some message while rejecting others considered 'undesirable' or perhaps not receivable. The differential reception of some signals through the filtering operations that result in further processing is not clearly understood. Presumably information from a channel to which the organism is 'tuned', despite the exposure to other channels, is processed further, remembered and used as a basis for a response. Challenges to this notion (Moray, 1959; Triesman, 1960; Gray and Wedderburn, 1960) have noted that there are psychological features associated with attention and not just physical characteristics, and that the content of a rejected message does leave an impression on the subject depending on the content of the rejected message and how it is presented to the subject. Material submitted to the 'wrong' ear produced a response from the subject. The information received by both ears will reach the same perceptual and discriminatory mechanisms involved (Deutsch and Deutsch, 1963). Sensory cues alone were found to be inadequate to explain the kind of selection going on when subjects receive information from several channels.

Modern linguistic theory does not address language competence and performance by reference to the above information processing activities. Hence whatever is called the comprehension of utterances requires extending the linguistic model to include explicit cognitive processes. Complex information processing goes on in selecting different channels and every incoming signal receives some kind of selective attention vis-à-vis its meaning by reference to memory storage and the sensory features of the incoming signals. Therefore, we must specify some of the complexities of attending to information whilst recognizing that we are capable of simultaneously generating several types of informational particulars.

Linguistic theory recognizes but does not address the fact that we make tacit use of information from visual and other sources when speaking, including thinking processes that enable us to expand utterance fragments into meaningful items because of culturally organized memory. This is not a matter of simple pattern recognition whereby the linguist could claim that sound patterns are organized by immediate and underlying rules in the act of reception. The shortcomings of any simple pattern match theory of reception can be clarified by examining the effects of context on the interpretation of letters, sentences, and visual appearances, where the same physical signals are interpreted quite differently when different surrounding contexts are introduced. Kolers and Pomerantz (1971) note that adult subjects create moving visual illusions from stationary stimuli that cannot be explained by *gestalt* principles or feature analysis extraction. Thus the contour of the stimuli are not primary, nor is any set of features said to index the stimuli presented. The interpretation of visual stimulus conditions seems to begin with a response to movement and is followed by the creation of recognizable patterns. The visual system is said to supplement inputs to it through cognitive organization and reorganization.

The processing of information seems to occur at several levels simultaneously despite the fact that our representation of what we are thinking, feeling, or perceiving is being channeled into a verbal coding that is oral and/or written and thus linear. This coding does not adequately represent the information we experience, but what we experience at different levels is important for what we say next to each other because our talk relies on this assumption.

The psychological model is not clear about how such cognitive processes are articulated with culture meanings that are negotiated in the setting. The processing presupposes that a pair of speaker-hearers are responding in a 'normal' way to informational particulars that can be seen as 'familiar' or 'normal' forms of everyday representations. But speaker-hearers must negotiate the discrepancy between what they may have stored in memory about substantive qualities of the everyday world and the variety of informational particulars available to their senses during social exchanges.

Multiple sources of information processed by different modalities limit what we learn in an interview. The limitations of cross modal information processing is especially difficult when we must rely on non-verbal communication. We have no way of discussing non-verbal communication (Cicourel in press [b]). What is at issue is the organism's ability to execute many disconnected conceptual processes simultaneously. Several points should be noted. (1) The difficulty of the tasks involved. (2) The number of events the subject can attend to and follow. (3) The respondent's ability to retain and retrieve variable amounts and types of information. (4) The subject's ability to organize and store experiences as socially meaningful chunks of information that can be accessed by reference to the original conditions of the experiences.

V. CONCLUSION

Traditional surveys with fixed-choice questions provide the respondent with a predigested decision process. After trial and error pre-tests with small samples of a population, questions are derived that are viewed as 'meaningful' to the larger representative target sample; the researcher has presumably narrowed the alternatives such that the questions are meaningful to the respondent's everyday experiences and faithful to the researcher's theory and hypotheses. The fixed-choice questionnaire is like the physician's medical history summary statement; the decision processes are not revealed to provide an independent reader with clues about its construction. The details of the decision processes that would clarify the reasoning on the part of the physician, and the reasoning attributed to the patient's answers, are not discernable to the reader. Survey questionnaires exhibit rather similar problems. Both procedures obscure the data base used for an analysis of the findings, or for justifying a suggested course of treatment or policy recommendations.

The survey researcher justifies his analysis of the coded responses by treating the interview problems as technical issues that can be resolved by interviewer training and standardized questions carefully formulated after one or more pre-tests. No information processing problem exists in this model of questions and answers. The physician assigns even less significance to interviewer training problems, despite devoting little time to formal monitoring of the kinds of questions formulated and the types of answers received from different patients. The physician relies on powerful theories from biology, biochemistry and the neuro-sciences to justify his diagnosis and treatment; he tends to ignore the difficult interface between the common sense talk to the patient, and the translation of the question-answer format into clinical science terms.

During interviewing we become aware of the general appearance of the respondent and the immediate informational particulars of what is being said by each party. The interviewer may simultaneously write things down, follow up a particular item, notice the next item, probe something the respondent has said, etc. Our attention may switch to objects in the setting and the movements the participant exhibits. Various features of the respondent may be noticed such as excessive perspiration, changes in skin color or texture, facial expressions, etc. These features may be noticed but not indexed in notes taken. The unrecorded information, however, can affect what is said next or at some later point in the interview, and may or may not be articulated with routine questions, or with the existing topic. Meanwhile, something like the prepossessing of a subroutine takes place while more formal questions are asked. These subroutines can lead to a preliminary diagnosis, additional unplanned questions, and a restructuring of subsequent parts of the interview. The summary statements of a medical history, therefore, selectively integrate various sources and types of information. The selective integration or processing during the interview is the basis for different question-answer subroutines, and produces condensed accounts or explanations that find their way into the medical history summary.

Fixed-choice questionnaire items seek to anticipate the natural processing of information that occurs in medical or similar interviews. This is done by forcing the respondents' experiences into a format that facilitates the analysis of coded responses. The analysis appears to be an obvious and straightforward cross-tabulation procedure involving different variables. The analysis implies an algorithm that contradicts the way humans normally receive and process questions and formulate possible answers. The survey researcher, therefore, ignores the ways humans normally ask questions and recognize appropriate answers in different cultural settings, treating the information processing activities as unremarkable.

In this paper I have tried to show how cognitive and linguistic or conversational elements are basic to the researcher's description of decision-making processes in interviews. These decision-making processes are of interest because their study helps to reveal some of the basic features that are associated with the prediction and interpretation of accounts in everyday life. Medical history interviewing was used to illustrate how medical knowledge glosses are produced. These glosses are based on the physician's brief written notes and his memory of the event. Details from a tape-recorded transcript was presented to illustrate how extensive information processing is used to negotiate the construction of a summary statement. The summary statement provides medical documentation for present and future treatment. The question-answer interview format used by the physician with a patient suggests how we can understand claims to knowledge that depend on the common sense reasoning inherent in this format.

University of California, San Diego

NOTE

* I am grateful to Lindsey Churchill, Jim Levin, and Hugh Mehan for a critical reading of the manuscript.

BIBLIOGRAPHY

Broadbent, D. E.: 1958 (reprint 1966), *Perception and Communication*, Pergamon, London.
Chase, W. G. and Simon, H. A.: 1973, 'Perception in Chess', *Cognitive Psychology* **4**, 55–81.
Cicourel, Aaron V.: in press (a), *Theory and Method in a Study of Argentine Fertility*, Wiley-Interscience, New York.
Cicourel, Aaron V.: in press (b), 'Gestural Sign Language and the Study of Non-Verbal Communication', I.C.A., London.
Deutsch, J. A. and Deutsch, D.: 1963, 'Attention: Some Theoretical Considerations', *Psychological Review* **70**, 80–90.
Gray, J. A. and Wedderburn, A. A.: 1960, 'Grouping Strategies with Simultaneous Stimuli', *Quarterly J. Experimental Psychology* **12**, 180–184.
Harrah, David: 1973, 'The Logic of Questions and its Relevance to Instructional Science', *Instructional Science* **1**, 447–467.
Hyman, H. H. *et al.*: 1954, *Interviewing in Social Research*, University of Chicago Press.
Kolers, Paul A. and Pomerantz, James R.: 1971, 'Figural Change in Apparent Motion', *J. of Experimental Psychology* **87**, 99–108.
Miller, George A.: 1956, 'The Magical Number Seven, Plus or Minus Two: Some Limits on Our Capacity for Processing Information', *Psychological Review* **63**, 81–97.
Moray, N.: 1959, 'Attention in Dichotic Listening: Affective Cues and the Influence of Instructions', *Quarterly J. Experimental Psychology* **11**, 56–60.
Neisser, U.: 1967, *Cognitive Psychology*, Appleton-Century-Crofts, New York.
Norman, Donald A.: 1969, *Memory and Attention*, Wiley, New York.
Norman, Donald A.: in press, 'Memory, Knowledge, and the Answering of Questions', in R. Solso (ed.), *The Loyola Symposium on Cognitive Psychology*, Winston, Washington, D.C..
Peirce, C. S.: 1957, *Essays in the Philosophy of Science* (ed. by Vincent Tomas), The Liberal Arts Press, New York.

Simon, H. A. and Barenfeld, M.: 1969, 'Information Processing Analysis of Perceptual Processes in Problem Solving', *Psychological Review* **76**, 473–483.

Triesman, A. M.: 1960, 'Contextual Cues in Selective Listening', *Quarterly J. Experimental Psychology* **12**, 242–248.

APPENDIX

I

Dr. X's Interview

(I = Interviewer, P = Patient)

(1) I: (unclear) How are you?

(2) P: Fine, thank you.

(3) I: I'm Dr. Huntley [as door is closed] and uh thanks for [slight laugh] undergoing your first interview. [sounds as if patient may have mumbled a low-keyed acknowledgment] (pause) Aas you know, uh and we're going ta re (slight pause) record this one because we're trying to get better ways of getting medical facts from patients (pause) in order to (slight pause) maybe get a more systematized approach to medical interview.

(4) P: Allright.

(5) I: So we get more information and consequently help you and other patients, better [P: low mumble like 'mmh'] and also we're teaching medical students how to talk to (slight pause) patients, so this is helpful too. That okay with you?

(6) P: Yes, that's fine [in low voice that sounds quite 'agreeable']

(7) I: Good (slight pause) great. (pause) Now let me have the history form you filled out.

(8) P: ↑I haven't

(9) I: That's alright, I'll go through it with you.

(10) P: And, yah, because some of them, you know, I put a question mark beside them, cause I'm [I: 'yah'] you know (pause)

(11) I: Why don't you just sit over there, I can talk to you better.

(12) P: $^\uparrow$You like
this one better [patient mumbling something here.]

(13) I: Get a big pillow (pause, movement of objects heard) get out
of the sun. Now just tell me your (slight pause) primary (slight
pause) problem that you want us to focus on. What is bothering
you at the moment?

(14) P: Well, Dr. B said I had high blood pressure. (pause)

(15) I: And this was just uh found routinely, uh [P: 'Well'] in the
course of an exam (book?) [patient tries to say something like
'I was pregnant'.] made to see Dr. B (slight pause) [patient and
Dr. talking simultaneously here] You were pregnant.

(16) P: That started it. I guess they thought it would go down (slight
pause) and uh (pause) it didn't.

(17) I: Now when was this first discovered? When were you pregnant?

(18) P: Well, I delivered in uh, uh, in June. (pause) I'd say. [I: 'okay'
said faintly.] I would say maybe, (slight pause) two and a half
months before.

(19) I: Two and a half months before or so perhaps [barely audible
here] sometime (unclear) in uh, uh time in March. And [cut off
by patient]

(20) P: Ohh about April [mumble afterwards]

(21) I: About April [P: mumbles something that from the tone of voice
sounds like agreement] Were you having any symptoms from
high blood pressure? (pause) Did you feel any different (slight
pause) other than having the pregnancy?

(22) P: Uhh (long pause) you know it looks like dust sometimes.

(23) I: I see. In other words, [patient starts to speak and stops] Your,
your vision isn't as clear as it should be.

(24) P: Well (pause) you see, this, now this is (pause) uhmm (slight
pause) a little, (pause) [sounds hesitant here] I'm supposed to
wear glasses. [I: 'yeah' said at same time as patients next word]

alright? And I have [pause] Uh, and I'ya (slight pause) just don't like to wear them because I have a small nose and they're down here constantly. (slight pause) I have [I: 'I see'] an oily complexion and all the rest. [I: 'mmh huh'] and uh (slight pause) they just don't work out. [the patient is sort of half laughing here and her manner of speaking is inarticulate.] So [laughs] (?) wearing them (?)

(25) I: Did you ever have any headaches, for example?

(26) P: Uh, I have occasional headaches, like I have a tension head-ache right now. [laughs here while saying something] (?) when (?) [since?] your secretary called yesterday.

(27) I: They all do, it's late in the afternoon.

(28) P: ↑It started, you know. It started. So uh [cut off by interviewer]

(29) I: What are the tension headaches like, (slight pause) what (slight pause) part of your scalp?

(30) P: ↑Like this, it hurts right over here.

(31) I: I see, over the right eye.

(32) P: Well, yes, this one (slight pause) feels [mumble by interviewer] yeah, but uh, (pause) and I, I, (slight pause) I happen [sounds like 'have'] to have them when my, when I menstruate or just before my period, or something. And this is what this one is like.

(33) I: You're how old now? 34? (P: '34' said simultaneously with interviewer) How long have you been having headaches of this sort?

(34) P: I don't have them anymore.

(35) I: Just occasionally? [faint something from patient that sounds like agreement] Every how often? (pause) one a month, once [patient cuts in]

(36) P: Not even once a month. (slight pause) I (long pause)

(37) I: Perhaps every once every two or three months (then uh?) (pause)

(38) P: You know, [interviewer: 'frequency or?'] well [well] let's say once every three months.

(39) I: Okay. [patient: 'Uhhh'] is it relieved by any medication? (slight pause) You, you take anything?

(40) P: ↑I take an aspirin sometimes (slight pause) that helps, and sometimes a dozen fails. Uhh, (slight pause) I'm not uh, I'm just about the opposite of other people (?) I don't like to see doctors. *Really* [interviewer: 'now don't scare me now' (?)] I don't, just don't like your profession [interviewer, with rising voice: 'Okay'] (pause) I'm just giving you fair warning.

(41) I: Right. I think people should stay away from doctors [laughs] (slight pause) unless it's absolutely essential. I couldn't agree with you more.

(42) P: Uh like I don't go in for pap smears when I'm supposed to (unclear) so do you? (?) I get extremely nervous about it. And I'm sure it upsets you, it's (?) my high blood pressure.

(43) I: Alright, I wouldn't be surprised. Since that's a (pause) common thing when people go to doctors, and when doctors go to doctors the same thing happens to them. [P: 'Does it?'] [Now they both talk simultaneously but the patient's remarks are not clear.] Oh sure their blood pressure goes up. [patient says something about 'a dentist friend who has high blood pressure' (pause) 'We're all (pause) basically human, you know'.] Now, (slight pause) when you have your headaches do you get sick to your stomach? [(pause) P: 'No'] (I think he says) that doesn't seem to be your problem. Okay, is your visual problem worse at the time? When you have your headaches (pause) do you see double or do you have blurring of vision?

(44) P: I've never had blurring I just, (slight pause) now when I was pregnant I did see those uhm white stars [I: 'I see'] you know

and I saw them one time I believe (said rather haltingly) and I've been looking for them then (slight pause) one time since I delivered and it was right soon after I had the baby (pause) but I haven't seen them I just see these little black, fuzzy looking things. Now whether it is due because I don't wear glasses or my eyes [interviewer breaks in] [can't understand patient]   ↑

(45) I: You mean you're even seeing them now or did they go away with each (patient breaks in)

(46) P: Oh, 1 see them occasionally [I: 'delivery'] (pause) yes uh [I: 'Okay'] sometimes I see them during the day, like I saw (slight pause) a couple this morning [I: 'mmh uhm'] but then right now I don't see any, and I'm looking for them and I don't see them.

(47) I: In both the right and left eye?

(48) P: More the left. [very long pause] [interviewer probably writing] [interviewer sort of coughs or clears throat]

(49) I: Now have you, do you have any idea how high your blood pressure levels were when Dr. B [patient interrupts here]

(50) P: ↑Oh, I know what it was the last time.

(51) I: What was it the last time?

(52) P: I believe he said 170 over 100.

(53) I: Okay, (slight pause) and when was that approximately? [P: 'hm'] This was after delivery or (interviewer mumbled something)

(54) P: Yeah, (slight pause) now this was (pause) the last visit I (pause) yeah, (slight pause) this was approximately a month ago.

(55) I: Okay, that's (slight pause) just fine, some time in July, just fine. Now (slight pause) how was the pregnancy, was it a routine pregnancy, was that your first or what number was it?

II

A. *The Initial Statement of the Medical History Summary*

Immediate Problem. The patient was first told of modest blood pressure elevation at age 31 when she consulted an American physician in Japan for palpitations and chest discomfort. Apparently the palpitations were related to emotional stress. An EKG was negative. Phenobarbital was prescribed. The physician noted that her blood pressure was 'up a little'.

B. *The Interview Dialogue upon which the Summary (II A) Was Based*

(93) I: Okay, now in terms of your blood pressure, uh, before you get back to that again, uh were you at any time in the past aware that your blood pressure was modestly elevated? Did any doctor tell you

(94) P: Just that (slight pause) fellow in Japan and he just didn't seem

(95) I: ↑during an exam

(96) P: to (?)

(97) I: ↑When was that, who was that fellow in Japan?

(98) P: Dr. G (patient and interviewer laugh)

(99) I: Your husband is in the military I gather.

(100) P: Yes, you know why (I: 'yeah') I uh, I, I thought you already asked me that because I (I: 'Right', (laughs slightly) because (?)) the girl in the other room asked me the same thing, I don't know his name (laughing) either.

(101) I: When were you, how old were you uh (pause) when you were in Japan? When you were in Japan at that time.

(102) P: (mumbling and unclear initially) I'd say three years ago.

(103) I: Okay, so you were about age 31, and uh, did you go on a routine (slight pause) check, but you don't go to doctors routinely. [P: 'no'] you must have had a complaint then. Why did you see Dr. G?

(104) P: ↑I did, I went in one Sunday afternoon because I felt like I was having pains in, and uh, and you know my heart, you know, (slight pause) was acting funny, so I had my husband take me in.

(105) I: Your heart was beating fast [P: 'yeah, and']

↑And you had some chest discomfort.

(106) P: So they did one of those (slight pause) those, things [I: 'electrocardiograms'] I believe (slight pause) with a little (pause) [unclear term] things like this.

(107) I: Right, and what did the doctor say?

(108) P: He said it looked alright.

(109) I: It looked okay.

(110) P: But he put me on uh (pause) phenobarbital; told me to come back the next day to see (pause) somebody else, [I: 'right'] general fellow and I went in and everything looked fine, so I said great forget it, you know (slight pause) and then I went in (slight pause) finally decided I'd better have (pause) [I: 'yeah'] (laughing here and unintelligible) and Dr. G. said it was up a little bit. (I: 'The uh' [cut off]) But he didn't say (hesitating here) that was all (pause) it was up a little bit.

(111) I: So once, twice when you saw Dr. G he found it to be (slight hesitation) up a little bit [P: 'no'] is that correct? or just the second time?

(112) P: ↑The first time I didn't see, yeah, I didn't see G the first time, (I: 'okay') I saw, just (slight pause) whoever was there, you know. Well, have you ever been in the Navy?

III

A. *A Further Statement of the Medical History Summary*

The patient was found to have modest elevation of blood pressure during the third trimester of her second pregnancy, which terminated 6/30/72 with normal delivery. During the third trimester of this pregnancy, or beginning about April 22nd, she had intermittent episodes of visual disturbance characterized as 'dust' appearing in the visual field. She described a fuzziness and occasional 'stars' flashing in the visual field. Such episodes are intermittent and brief in duration. At no time did she have difficulty focusing, scotomata, or double vision. No cardiorespiratory, renal problems, or evidence of eclampsia complicated the last pregnancy. In the post-partum check, she was still found to be modestly hypertensive, the last check being in July of '72, at which time the BP was in the range of 170/70.

Headaches: For several years, probably longer, she has been subjected to recurrent headaches. These are related to tension and also the onset of her menses. These take the form of a dull discomfort, usually over one or the other eye in the frontal region and are readily relieved with aspirin; duration 1–2 hours. No associated photophobia, nausea, vomiting. These are not in the migraine pattern.

B. *The Interview Dialogue upon which the Summary (III A) Was Based*

(11) I: Why don't you just sit over there, I can talk to you better.

(12) P: ↑You like this one better [patient mumbling something here.]

(13) I: Get a big pillow (pause, movement of objects heard) get out of the sun. Now just tell me your (slight pause) primary (slight pause) problem that you want us to focus on. What is bothering you at the moment?

(14) P: Well, Dr. B said I had high blood pressure. (pause)

(15) I: And this was just uh found routinely, uh [P: 'Well'] in the course of an exam (book?) [patient tries to say something like 'I was pregnant'.] made to see Dr. B (slight pause) [patient and Dr. talking simultaneously here] You were pregnant.

(16) P: That started it. I guess they thought it would go down (slight pause) and uh (pause) it didn't.

(17) I: Now when was this first discovered? When were you pregnant?

(18) P: Well, I delivered in uh, uh, in June. (pause) I'd say. [I: 'okay' said faintly.] I would say maybe, (slight pause) two and a half months before.

(19) I: Two and a half months before or so perhaps [barely audible here] sometime (unclear) in uh, uh time in March. And [cut off by patient]

(20) P: Ohh about April [mumble afterwards]

C. *Further Dialogue Used for the Summary (III A)*

(21) I: About April [P: mumbles something that from the tone of voice sounds like agreement] Were you having any symptoms from high blood pressure? (pause) Did you feel any different (slight pause) other than having the pregnancy?

(22) P: Uhh (long pause) you know it looks like dust sometimes.

(23) I: I see. In other words, [patient starts to speak and stops] Your, your vision isn't as clear as it should be.

(24) P: Well (pause) you see, this, now this is (pause) uhmm (slight pause) a little, (pause) [sounds hesitant here] I'm supposed to wear glasses. [I: 'yeah' said at same time as patients next word] alright? And I have [pause] uh, and I'ya (slight pause) just don't like to wear them because I have a small nose and they're down here constantly. (slight pause) I have [I: 'I see'] an oily complexion and all the rest. [I: 'mmh huh'] and uh (slight pause) they just don't work out. [the patient is sort of half laughing here and her manner of speaking is inarticulate.] So [laughs] (?) wearing them (?)

(25) I: Did you ever have any headaches, for example?

D. *Further Dialogue Used for the Summary (III A)*

(26) P: Uh, I have occasional headaches, like I have a tension headache right now. [laughs here while saying something] (?) when (?) [since?] your secretary called yesterday.

(27) I: They all do, it's late in the afternoon.

(28) P: ↑It started, you know. It started. So uh [cut off by interviewer]

(29) I: What are the tension headaches like, (slight pause) what (slight pause) part of your scalp?

(30) P: ↑Like this, it hurts right over here.

(31) I: I see, over the right eye.

(32) P: Well, yes, this one (slight pause) feels [mumbles by interviewer] yeah, but uh, (pause) and I, I, (slight pause) I happen [sounds like 'have'] to have them when my, when I menstruate or just before my period, or something. And this is what this one is like.

(33) I: You're how old now? 34? (P: '34' said simultaneously with interviewer) How long have you been having headaches of this sort?

(34) P: I don't have them anymore.

SOLOMON MARCUS

FIFTY-TWO OPPOSITIONS BETWEEN SCIENTIFIC AND POETIC COMMUNICATION

Scientific and poetic communication are two forms of a more general type of human communication, belonging to the family of languages of discovery. So, there are many common features between them. This is just the reason why it is interesting to investigate the differences, the oppositions between these two types of communication. Trubetzkoy has pointed out that oppositions between relatively similar things are more interesting than oppositions between completely different things [27]. So, in English it is more interesting to study the opposition between the phonemes s and z, which are similar except for one feature (nonvoiced-voiced) then the opposition between s and n, which differ with respect to several features (strident-nonstrident, nonnasal-nasal, continuant-noncontinuant, nonvoiced-voiced).

We deal in the following with two idealized types of communication, as two terms of reference, two coordinate axes, with respect to which real human communication finds its position. So, no concrete scientific communication is a prototype of Scientific Communication (SC) and no concrete poetic communication is a prototype of Poetic Communication (PC). The idealized scientific communication we are concerned with is in fact an idealized type of mathematical communication.

Our base of discussion will be a list of oppositions between SC and PC. Some of them have been proposed long ago, but perhaps we argue about them in a new order of ideas; others are added by us, which were discussed, to a great extent, in some of our previous papers. There is a third class of oppositions which we try to prove are (at least partially) wrong, although many authors assert them.

Scientific communication	*Poetic communication*
(1) Rational.	Emotional
(2) Explicable.	Ineffable.
(3) Lucidity.	Enchantment.

C. Cherry (ed.), Pragmatic Aspects of Human Communication, 83–96. All Rights Reserved
Copyright © 1974 by D. Reidel Publishing Company, Dordrecht-Holland

(4) General and universal meanings.　Singular and local meanings.

(5) Objective meanings.　Subjective meanings.

(6) Fixity in space (independence with respect to the reader or listener).　Variability in space (dependence with respect to the listener).

(7) Constancy in time.　Variability in time.

(8) Dominated by the man.　Dominates the man.

(9) Use of artificial expressions.　Exclusive use of expressions of natural languages.

(10) Essential rôle of artificial expressions.　Secondary rôle of artificial expressions.

(11) Routin use of the language (all linguistic means have a conventional character).　Creative use of the language (tendency to linguistic innovation).

(12) Transparence (the language is only a window through which we look at the scientific meanings).　Opacity (the window is black, it stops our look and becomes an aim in itself).

(13) Transitive (the scientific meanings are able to be communicated to another one).　Intransitive (poetic meanings have the tendency to be directed toward the poet himself).

(14) Logical density (syllogisms and deductions are more dense in SC than in the every day language).　Density of suggestion (in PC things are not called by their usual name, but by means of some intermediate objects).

(15) Vanishing of language (the language is forgotten after we perceive its semantic content).　Persistance of language (the language cannot be separated from its semantic content).

(16) Translatable.　Untranslatable.

(17) Relative independence with respect to the expression.　Strong dependence with respect to the expression.

(18) Relative independence with respect to the musical structure.　Strong dependence with respect to the musical structure.

(19) Preponderance of the paradigmatic aspects.　Preponderance of the syntagmatic aspects.

(20) Short contexts are enough to determine the semantics (tendency to context free).

Poetic semantics need large contexts (tendency to increase the context sensitive character).

(21) Preponderance of conceptual (definitional) meanings.

Preponderance of non-conceptual (contextual) meanings.

(22) Written character.

Oral character.

(23) Infinite synonymy (for each string x there are infinitely many strings having the same meaning as x).

Lack of synonymy (impossibility of two strings having a common meaning).

(24) Lack of homonymy (closing).

Infinite homonymy (opening) of each string.

(25) Existence of semantically null strings.

Non-existence of semantically null strings.

(26) Denumerability of the set of meanings.

Noncountability of the set of meanings.

(27) Discreteness of the set of meanings.

Continuity of the set of meanings.

(28) Concordance between the cardinal of the set of expressions and the cardinal of the set of meanings (both are denumerable).

Contradiction between the cardinal of the set of expressions and the cardinal of the set of meanings (the former is denumerable, whereas the latter has the power of the continuum).
Existence of essential ambiguities.

(29) Possibility of solving any ambiguity by passing either to a higher level of abstraction or to a larger context.

(30) General and conventional stereotypes.

Particular and original stereotypes.

(31) Denotation (tendency to use all meanings following a dictionary).

Connotation (tendency to use the expressions in a sense other than their basic sense).

(32) Existence of the problems of style (the choice between synonymic strings).

Absence of the problems of style (in the sense of classical Rhetorics).

(33) Essential use of metaphors.

Nonessential use of metaphors.

(34) There exists no opposition of the metaphor with a non-expressive term.

The metaphoric function is fulfilled in opposition with a non-expressive term.

(35) Homogeneity of some metaphors (both terms between which the analogy is considered belong to the same language: the mathematical language).

Heterogeneity of all metaphors (one term belongs to the every-day language, whereas the other belongs to the poetic language).

(36) Possibility of metaphors of a higher degree (a metaphor of degree n is the result of an analogy with a metaphor of degree $n-1$).

Impossibility of metaphors of degree greater than 1.

(37) Relevance of the opposition *true-false* (in the sense of bivalent logic).

Non-relevance of the opposition *true-false*.

(38) Relevance of the opposition *grammatical-nongrammatical*.

Non-relevance of the opposition *grammatical-nongrammatical*.

(39) Use of formal systems in order to study wellformed strings.

Use of formal systems in order to study various degrees of 'nonwell-formedness'.

(40) Great paradigmatic distance implies great syntagmatic distance.

Short syntagmatic distances associated with great paradigmatic distances.

(41) Short paradigmatic distance implies short syntagmatic distance.

Great syntagmatic distances associated with short paradigmatic distances.

(42) Non-relevance of Roman Jakobson's thesis [9].

Validity of Jakobson's thesis concerning the projection of equivalence principle from the axis of selection onto the axis of combination [9].

(43) Tendency to metaphor.

Tendency to metonymy.

(44) Tendency to iconic signs.

Tendency to symbolic signs.

(45) Centred over the context.

Centred over the message.

(46) High degree of predictability.	Low degree of predictability.
(47) Non-relevance of the informational analogy to the Second Principle of Thermodynamics.	Relevance of the informational analogy to the Second Principle of Thermodynamics (in the sense of [23], [11] and [1]).
(48) Logical-algebraical character of the structured Semantics.	Topological character of the structured Semantics.
(49) Importance of the extra-linguistic context.	Tendency to use the linguistic context only.
(50) Syntactic projectivity of most strings (if a term a in a string is subordinated to another term b, then any intermediate term is subordinated to b).	Tendency to increase the number of nonprojective strings.
(51) Fulfilment of the Tesnière property (every term is dependent on at most one other term).	Existence of many sentences which do not fulfil the Tesnière property.
(52) Normal distance between the governing and the dependent elements.	Large distance or small distance between the governing and the dependent elements.

Opposition 1, although asserted by most authors, is simply false. There are emotions which have nothing to do with the poetic communication and, on the other side, only lyric poetry is centred over the addresser, i.e. it is dominated by the emotion. Roman Jakobson proposed to define the poetic function of human communication as that centred over the message and this idea leads us to the opposition 45 (see [9]). But, if we accept this proposal, we obtain the paradoxical fact that any game with words is the best manifestation of the poetic function, although such a game may have nothing to do with poetry. Algebraic calculations are also sometimes centred over themselves, yet they are a pure manifestation of scientific communication.

Opposition 2 seems to be also partially false. Even in SC there are things which are not explicable at a given moment. Gödel's theory (concerning the impossibility of obtaining a complete formalization of Arithmetics) points out the 'ineffable' of one of the most rigourous fields of science. This fact makes wrong to some extent the oppositions 3, 8 and 11. But 3 is partially true in view of 4; the singular and local character of poetic meanings require a state of enchantment; manipulations of meanings are never a routine in PC. Opposition 8 follows from 23, which is perhaps the most important, because definitions and proofs in SC require, for any string, infinitely many equivalent strings, whereas no semantic equivalent strings exist in PC. Thus, the source of 23 is to a great extent given by the oppositions 14 and 21; only with conceptual (definitional) meanings can we perform syllogistic proofs (in essence this opposition is due to Pius Servien [26]; see also [12] and [14] for a more detailed explanation). The conceptual-contextual opposition between SC and PC is explained in more details in [19] and [20]. SC is dominated by the man just in this sense: the man can always choose one of infinitely many possibilities to express a given scientific meaning. On the other hand, no such choice exists in PC, every expression is imposed here by its meaning; so PC dominates the man, leaves him no freedom. Thus, 8 is partially true and 32 is completely true; indeed, in the sense of classical rhetorics the problem of style is always concerned with the question 'How to say?' and never with the question 'What to say?' From 23 follow 16, 17 and 18. Translation from the language L_1 into the language L_2 is a process of finding in L_2 synonymic strings of strings in L_1 and this is always possible in SC, because the set of synonymic strings of a given string in SC has representants in every natural language. Opposition 17 is only relative, because no definite expression is required for a scientific meaning, although any scientific meaning requires expressions. The same situation arises in 18; in [12] it is proved that there exist infinitely many different rhythmic structures for expressing the same scientific meaning; but, of course, any scientific meaning requires a rhythmic structure.

Another clue-opposition is 24, which is only an approximation of the more sophisticated opposition 29. There are, of course, local ambiguities in SC: the word 'category' (which has about four different meanings in Mathematics), the use of 'variables' like $x, f, \langle X, \tau \rangle$ at different levels of abstraction (the level of arguments, the level of functions, the level of topological spaces, etc). The ambiguity of the value $f_1(x)$ when $x \in [a, b]$ is resolved by passing to the function f_1; the ambiguity of the notation f when it is an arbitrary real continuous function defined on $[a, b]$ is resolved by passing to the space $G([a, b])$ of continuous functions on $[a, b]$.

The ambiguity of 'category' is resolved by means of the context. Elements like x and f are the 'shifters' of the mathematical language, like personal pronouns and time or position adverbs in natural languages. In PC there are a lot of local ambiguities which can be resolved at the level of a whole poem or of the whole work of a poet. But many ambiguities are essential in PC, which can be neither avoided nor solved. There are two reasons for this fact, one related to the inner structure of PC (see [24]), another related to the feed-back character of PC (opposition 5). This feed-back character of PC is a result of the so-called valuation-structure associated with PC and determined by the oppositions 6 and 7. For an exact explanation of this matter, see [12]. The inner structure of PC involves a high degree of ambiguity (more exactly: of polysemy) in view of its connotative character; thus 31 is a basic opposition (see an exact explanation of it at pp. 310–311 of [15]), which unfortunately is often confounded with the opposition nonmetaphorical-metaphorical. As a matter of fact, most metaphors are denotative and many connotations have nothing to do with metaphors. We have proved in [13] the essential rôle of metaphors in the mathematical language, which is purely denotative. On the other side, modern poetry is needy of metaphors. Metaphors cannot be missing in SC, because they are required by the process of generalization and abstraction of science and by the heuristic function of mathematical language, requiring us to give similar names to similar things. Thus, we have opposition 33 and, as was explained in [13], oppositions 34 and 35. There is a kind of *stability* about the SC where, to small modifications of the things correspond small modifications of the names of these things (like continuity-semicontinuity, $\sum$ and $\int$, 0 and $\emptyset$, $\cup$ and $\vee$) and this leads to the concept of semimetaphor (see [13]). Colin Cherry observes ([4], p. 74) that "after continued use, many metaphorical words become incorporated into the language and lose their original significance; words such as 'explain', 'ponder' 'see (what you mean)' we no longer think of as metaphorical". There is thus a process of transformation of poetic metaphors into linguistic metaphors. Something similar (but not identical) happens with the mathematical metaphor. Its evolution is in the opposite sense; rather than degenerate, it generates new mathematical metaphors, of a higher degree: metaphors, metaphors of metaphors, metaphors of metaphors of metaphors etc. "Metaphors arise because we continually need to stretch the range of words as we accumulate new concepts and abstract relationships", says Colin Cherry in [4], p. 74 (see also [5]). In [13] we gave concrete analysis of such processes of generation of mathematical metaphors of higher degree. There is no possibility of a poetical metaphor of a higher degree, because once a poetical metaphor of second degree is born, the corresponding poetical metaphor of first degree is no longer a poetical, but a linguistic metaphor. Thus, we have opposition 37.

Related to 33, 34 and 35 are the oppositions 43 and 44. Classical poetry, as classical art, were based on the principle of mimesis, whereas modern poetry and modern art are very indirectly related to the objects of the real world and even this weak relation between art and real objects is more a matter of contiguity than a matter of analogy. On the other side, SC uses more and more metaphors in view of its high degree of generalization; we have now in Mathematics very many words from Botany, Medicine and from every day life. In their classical work [22], Ogden and Richards distinguish between the symbolic and the emotive uses of language, but for us 'symbolic' is opposed not to 'emotive', but to 'iconic'. As Colin Cherry observed in [4], p. 75 "many scientific words perform the symbolic function" ... whereas ([4], p. 76) "poetry may largely dispense with such symbolic, logical use of words". But ([4], p. 76) "these two 'polar extremes' of the whole sphere of language, the symbolic and emotive, which we may in extreme call the scientific and the aesthetic, are not mutually exclusive and antagonistic. In all speech and writing, something of both uses is called into play". These were written by Colin Cherry in 1957. Our above oppositions 43 and 44 come against opposition 1 and against the point of view of classical Art and classical Mathematics, as it is reflected in the above quotations. Some tendencies of contemporary abstract art and of modern mathematics were not clear enough 15 years ago, but they are clear now and this is the reason of our proposition to modify the classical oppositions between science and art. An important intermediate step in this process of clearing up was the opposition 45 proposed essentially by Roman Jakobson. But, as we have seen, this opposition too requires a reconsideration, toward a more shaded representation of the differences between SC and PC.

Oppositions 14, 23, 24, 9, 16, 32, 4, 5, 6, 7, 26, 27, 28, 12, 13, 17, 18, 19, 40, 41, 42 are argued, exactly in this order, in [14]. Oppositions 20, 37, 31, 11, 30, 2, 46, 47 are argued in [15]. Oppositions 25, 15 and again

40, 41 and 42 are argued in [16]. Opposition 22 was pointed out by Leonard Bloomfield in [2]. Perhaps it would be better to replace it by "the exclusive written character of the SC – the essential oral and written character of the PC". Indeed, poetry has a polydimensional organization (in verses, strophes, etc.), it has a spatial written organization (see Apollinaire and the so-called concrete poetry or spatial poetry) and these visual phenomena cannot be always translated into auditory structures. We miss something when we replace reading of poetry by listening to poetry.

A few comments should be made about the opposition 39. Formal systems (beginning with Hilbert) are a way to investigate the structure of theorems, i.e. of strings which are well formed from a logical point of view. Beginning with Chomsky, formal systems like some combinatorial systems and some types of automata are used in the investigation of strings which are well formed from a grammatical point of view. But the wellformedness of a string is always a relative property. A string is a theorem with respect to a determined choice of axioms and of rules of deduction: it is a grammatical string with respect to a given generative grammar. A given level of wellformedness is important as a purely conventional term of reference, in the comparative investigation of various types of strings which are not wellformed, just as is the choice of an origin and of a unit of measure, when we want to compare the relative positions of points on a straight line. This is just the aim of formal systems in the study of poetic language, where the poetic figures are given by various levels of semi-truth and semi-grammaticality (oppositions 37 and 38) i.e. by various types of strings which are not wellformed. This is, essentialy, the difficult problem of measurement of various degrees of connotativity and we have tried to give some partial answers to it in Chapters V and VII of [17].

Many authors claim that the opposition 46 gives a basical difference between scientific and aesthetic communication. This idea has perhaps its origin in a very known principle which asserts that poetry is based on a frustrated waiting: this frustrated waiting implies an aggrandizement of the indetermination of the aesthetic message. This is entirely true, if we have in view especially the bold poetic figures of modern poetry, but this is only one aspect of the matter. There is another tendency, which works exactly in the opposite sense, a tendency to diminish the indetermination by means of a very strong global organization of the aesthetic works. A poem, for instance, is the result of a two level process, which consists of a great number of local disorders (with respect to the order of the everyday language) implying an aggrandizement of the indetermination and an order of second degree of a purely global nature, which brings forth a magic coherence of the whole text and implies a reduction of the indetermination. These two contradictory tendencies act in different degrees in any poetic text and the result must be tested everytime by a special investigation. The various possibilities of improving the measure of information by taking into account more and more semantic information are discussed in Chapter VI in [4]. MacKay distinguishes between selective and semantic information and he claims that selective information (i.e. the information necessary to select the message itself from a possible set of messages) may be separated from the semantic information [10]. Charles Morris claims that "information of the Shannon variety is selective information only and has nothing to do with the signification of the message" ([21], p. 64).

If opposition 46 fails, it seems to us that opposition 47 is more adequate to the linguistic reality of the texts. The informational 'energy' (in the sense of [23]) is correlated to the informational entropy (i.e. 'indetermination') by means of a theorem which gives the linguistic analogy of the Second Principle of Thermodynamics (see [1] and [11]). But this informational analogy of the Second Principle of Thermodynamics expresses an orientation, a function of the text, only when the text is an aim in itself, as in a poetic discourse.

Opposition 48 is, in our opinion, one of the deepest differences between SC and PC. The very quantified nature of the semantics in SC implies its logical-algebraical character, the possibility of using logical semantics and various algebraic calculations when dealing with scientific meanings. Quite different is the situation with poetic meanings. The neighbourhood of such a meaning cannot be described by means of a distance. The connotative nature of PC on one hand, the way in which the listener influences and modifies the poetic meaning on the other hand imply a topological structure organically related to PC. We don't want to enter here into technical details concerning the nature and the significance of these topologies; they may be found in [12], where the topology is required by the openness, the polysemy, of PC, and in [24], where the topology is required by the connotative nature of PC. All these topological structures belong to General Topology. There is another order of ideas, which involves, in the description of PC, some techniques belonging to Algebraic Topology, more exactly to Homology Theory. This way was proposed by Walther L. Fischer [6], [7].

Opposition 49 is a refined formulation of opposition 45, but it must be emphasised that the word 'context' has a different meaning in 45 with respect to 49. In 45 we use the word context in the Jakobsonian sense of reality, situation, i.e., extralinguistic context. Thus, PC is every time a new language, where most morphemes (especially lexical morphemes) lose their referential meaning, their dictionary meaning, and try to take on new connotations. But the exclusivity of the linguistic context is not characteristic of PC; the language LINCOS by Freudenthal, devoted to cosmic intercourse, uses only purely syntactical means to define its meanings, but it has nothing to do with Poetry [8], [19].

The above discussion shows that there are two various degrees of validity among the fifty two oppositions quoted at the beginning of this paper. Oppositions like 1 and 46 are wrong in the sense that they are concerned with features which don't really belong to SC any more than to PC (rational, high degree of predictability) or to PC more than to SC (emotional, low degree of predictability). Oppositions 45 and 49 are wrong in a quite different sense, in fact they are less wrong than 1 and 46. Oppositions 45 and 49 are concerned with features which really belong to SC more than to PC, and to PC more than to SC, respectively, but they are not characteristic of them. But in this respect we must be aware that no opposition alone, not any small group of oppositions, are enough to detect the complexity of the structure of SC and PC. The above list of 52 oppositions is open to modifications and additions, because no finite set of oppositions gives conditions which are both necessary and sufficient for human communication to be SC or PC. See [18] for a systematic and detailed explanation of the oppositions 50, 51 and 52.

A glance at the 52 oppositions above, between SC and PC, shows the great number of *similarities* between SC and PC: use of natural languages, great density, ambiguity, stereotypy, use of metaphors, use of formal systems as a tool in their investigation, systematic relation between the paradigmatic and the syntagmatic distance, mathematical structure of the Semantics, existence of a creativity under the form of a finite set of rules. Just this common basis increases the interest of oppositions between SC and PC. An old and deep study of the similarities between SC and PC is given in [3].

An important question is this: to what extent do the oppositions above remain valid when we replace PC by Artistic Communication (AC). The features of AC will be those features which belong to *any* type of artistic communication (PC is thus a particular form of AC). Oppositions 1–8, 11–13, 15, 17, 19–21, 23–27, 29–30, 32–33, 36–39, 43–46, 48–49 need no supplementary explanation; they remain valid as such, when we replace PC by AC. Oppositions 9 and 10 have no sense before explaining what 'artificial' and 'natural' could mean in painting or in music, for instance. This is an open question. Opposition 14 makes no sense, because there is no musical name of the objects; so, in painting, or in music, suggestion is confused by the use of symbolic signs and opposition 14 is replaced by the opposition 44.

Again, opposition 16 makes no sense, because it is not clear what kind of translatability we are dealing with in painting for instance.

Opposition 18 makes no sense either, because there is no sonorous structure in painting, for instance. There is no oral character of painting, so we have to abandon opposition 22 too. In painting, the expression is continuous as well as the semantics, so there is no contradiction between the cardinal of the set of expressions and the cardinal of the set of meanings; thus opposition 28 is no longer valid. The distinction between basic meaning and secondary meaning makes no sense, neither in music nor in painting, because there is no referential dictionary: so the opposition 31 between denotation and connotation has no more sense. We don't know what is meant by the 'nonexpressive' term when dealing with music or with painting, nor is there any everyday musical or pictural language; so oppositions 34 and 35 need further investigations. Such concepts as 'paradigmatic' and 'syntagmatic distance' tacitly assume a discrete and linear character of the artistic expression, but this condition is not fulfilled with respect to painting. We can hope that the so-called picture grammars (see, for instance, the recent book by Rosenfeld [25]) will give essential help in this respect, so that oppositions 40, 41, 42 and 47 will become clarified.

A similar situation arises with oppositions 50, 51, and 52; they require a discrete and linear character of artistic expression.

Let us add that SC and PC are not ideal in the axiologic sense, but from the point of view of their abstract form. Mallarmé is nearer to PC than Apollinaire, without being greater.
I wish to thank Professor Colin Cherry for his comments, helping me to improve this article.

Institute of Mathematics,
Bucharest, Roumania

BIBLIOGRAPHY

[1] R. W. Bailey, 'Statistics and the Sounds of Poetry', *Poetics, International Review for the Theory of Literature*, Vol. 1, 16–37, Mouton, The Hague-Paris.
[2] L. Bloomfield, *Linguistic Aspects of Science*, International Encyclopedia of Unified Science, Vols. I and II: *Foundations of the Unity of Science* 1, No. 4, The University of Chicago Press, 1939; 10th ed., 1969, p. 7.
[3] S. Buchanan, *Poetry and Mathematics*, The John Day Company, New York, 1929.
[4] C. Cherry, *On Human Communication (A Review, a Survey and a Criticism)* (2nd ed.), MIT Press, Cambridge, Mass. 1966.
[5] J. R. Davitz (ed.), *The Communication of Emotional Meaning*, Mc Graw-Hill, New York and London 1964.
[6] W. L. Fischer, 'Topologische Stilcharakteristiken von Texten', *Grundlagenstudien aus Kybernetik und Geisteswissenschaft* 10 (1969) 111–119.
[7] W. L. Fischer, 'Beispiele für topologische Stilcharakteristiken von Texten', *Grundlagenstudien aus Kybernetik und Geisteswissenschaft* 11 (1970) 1–11.
[8] H. Freudenthal, *Lincos, Design for a Language for Cosmic Intercourse*, North-Holland Publishing Company, Amsterdam, 1960.
[9] R. Jakobson, 'Linguistics and Poetics', *Style in Language* (ed. by T. Sebeok), MIT Press, Cambridge, Mass., 1960; 2nd Paperback Printing, 1968, pp. 350–377.
[10] D. M. MacKay, 'In Search of Basic Symbols' and 'The Nomenclature of Information Theory', *Cybernetics: Transactions of the Eighth Congress* (ed. by H. von Foerster), Macy Foundation, New York, 1952.
[11] S. Marcus, 'Entropie et énergie poétique', *Cahiers de linguistique théorique et appliquée* 4 (1967) 171–180.
[12] S. Marcus, 'Langage scientifique, structures rythmiques, langage lyrique', *Cahiers de Linguistique Théorique et Appliquée* 5 (1968) 127–158.
[13] S. Marcus, 'The Metaphors of the Mathematical Language', *Revue Roumaine des Sciences Sociales. Série de Philosophie et Logique* 14 (1970) 139–145.
[14] S. Marcus, 'Two Poles of the Human Language. I', *Revue Roumaine de Linguistique* 15 (1970) 187–198.
[15] S. Marcus, 'Two Poles of the Human Language. II', *Revue Roumaine de Linguistique* 15 (1970) 309–316.
[16] S. Marcus, 'Two Poles of the Human Language. III', *Revue Roumaine de Linguistique* 15 (1970) 495–500.
[17] S. Marcus, *Poetica matematică*, Editura Academiei, Bucuresti, 1970.

[18] S. Marcus, 'Trois types d'écarts syntaxiques et trois types de figures dans le langage poétique', *Cahiers de Linguistique Théorique et Appliquée* **7** (1970) 181–187.

[19] S. Marcus, 'Semnificatie de dictionar si Semnificatie de Context', *Educatie si Limbaj*, Editura didactică si pedagogică, Bucuresti, 1972, pp. 63–70.

[20] S. Marcus, 'Conceptual and Contextual Hypostasieses of Abstract Entities', The Session of Roumanian Academy devoted to *The Statute of Abstract Entities, April 1972*, The Publishing House of the R.S.R. Academy, Bucharest, 1973.

[21] C. Morris, *Signification and Significance*, MIT Press, Cambridge, Mass., 1964, pp. 62–64.

[22] C. K. Ogden and I. A. Richards, *The Meaning of Meaning*, Routledge and Kegan Paul Ltd., London, 1949 (1st ed., 1923).

[23] O. Onicescu, 'Energie informationnelle', *Comptes Rendus de l'Académie des Sciences, Paris*, Serie A **263** (1966) 841–842.

[24] I. I. Revzin, 'The Continuous Nature of the Poetic Semantics', to appear in *Poetics, International Review for the Theory of Literature*, No. 10, 1974.

[25] A. Rosenfeld, *Picture Processing by Computer*, Academic Press, New York-London, 1969.

[26] P. Servien, *Le Langage des Sciences*, Blanchard, Paris, 1931.

[27] N. S. Trubetzkoy, *Principes de Phonologie* (transl. from German by J. Cantineau), Paris, 1957.

MERRILL GARRETT

EXPERIMENTAL ISSUES
IN SENTENCE COMPREHENSION:
COMPLEXITY AND SEGMENTATION*

ABSTRACT. Questions about the order of processing events during speech perception are among the most interesting and challenging in the psychology of language. Relating segmentation strategies to computational effort appears to be a possible approach to a difficult area. If we knew where processing takes place and where it is held in abeyance, we would have some basis for inferring what kinds of information are needed by the recognition system for the projection of grammatical structures. Knowing what kinds of structures are, in fact, inferred by the hearer at given points in the sentence would help us to refine our guesses about the function of specific kinds of information (e.g., acoustic, phonetic, lexical, etc.).

Three working hypotheses about order of processing are offered with some research relevant to each. The experiments reported here are by no means sufficient to establish the hypotheses offered. They may serve to illustrate some of the ways to pursue research which could decide such issues.

It will be useful to outline the notion of comprehension assumed in this discussion before addressing any experimental issues. It is primarily a syntactic notion defined on sentences. Of course, the problem of language comprehension is more general than the problem of understanding a sentence. In part, the decision to focus on sentences as units of analysis stems from a conviction that the psychological mechanisms needed to account for the integration of information from two or more distinct surface sentences will be very similar to those that account for our ability to integrate the information from the different underlying sentences of a single complex surface sentence. The generality of the features of sentence comprehension that interest us may become apparent after we somewhat sharpen the notion of 'sentence understanding'.

I. WHAT HAPPENS WHEN WE 'UNDERSTAND SENTENCES'?

The phrase 'understanding a sentence' is quite vague, and yet most readers have probably so far accepted it without discomfort – indeed, have probably felt they 'understood' it when first encountered above. This illustrates an important fact about normal sentence understanding: namely, that we seem content to operate much of the time with what can fairly easily be shown to be a partial understanding of the meaning of the utterances with which we are confronted.

This is, of course, not an unusual insight. As everyone has had occasion to note, we often need little more than a partial understanding of what is addressed to us in order to cope satisfactorily. Though I do not wish to pursue the point at length, it seems an entirely defensible thesis that we understand only so much of sentences as suits our temporary purpose, and that this is nothing short of a virtue. We extract certain information about the structure and meaning of the uttereances that we hear and are content to await both the occasion and the necessity of a more precise interpretation of those sentences. What is being emphasized is that the inference of a structure for a sentence may be distinct from its interpretation in any extended sense. For example, if we take a complex sentence like, *John is taller than Bob, who is shorter than Sam*, and then ask the question, 'who is smallest?', most people will be given a moment's pause. Nevertheless, there is a very reasonable sense in which someone who may have momentary difficulty in answering such a question may be said to have understood the sentence being questioned.

What then *are* the aspects of sentence structure that must be specified if we are to claim that sentence comprehension has taken place in the minimal sense? In the broadest terms, there are two: the *segments* of the string and the grammatical *relations* which hold among them.

Evidently, the first process is the translation of the acoustic event into a set of discrete, meaning-bearing elements. This condition could be expressed in a variety of technical ways but, for present purposes, it is sufficient to require that there be some translation of the acoustic signal into a sequence of words.

The second aspect of the interpretive activity must involve establishing a set of relations which hold among those words. These relations are of two sorts: (1) relations which hold among the words belonging to the *same* underlying simple sentence (*sentoid*), and (2) relations which hold among the sentoids that make up a complex sentence. It is important to understand that these relations are *not* the same as those distinguished by surface structure and deep structure descriptions; both sets of relations are defined over deep structure. The relations within a sentoid are, for example, subject of a verb, object of a verb, etc.; the relations between sentoids can be characterized in terms of the embedding types to be found in natural languages; namely, conjunction, relativization, and complementation.

Thus, we expect a minimal characterization of a sentence for its comprehension to be a translation of the acoustic signal into a sequence of words, the assignment of each of those words to one or more sentoids, and the stipulation of grammatical relations holding among words and among sentoids. That is a very modest list. It is very much a semantically or interpretively oriented list, and yet it also directly relates to what are commonly thought of as syntactic properties of sentences.

Note that, although these are structural properties upon which a *meaning* could be elaborated, they do not specify which aspects of the detailed *syntactic* structure of a sentence are in fact elaborated. For instance, a good deal of bracketing information that is ordinarily represented in the surface structure of a sentence need not be a part of the characterization just outlined. The specification of what modifies what, of what the relations are between sentoids, etc., will have consequences for the surface bracketing of a sentence, but does not fully determine the surface structure. A variety of surface structures may be contingent on such grammatical relations.

The notion of understanding a sentence that emerges from this view is not the construction at each moment of a complete and precise structure which characterizes the entire syntactic and semantic properties of a sentence as they would be provided by an adequate grammar of a language; rather it characterizes the understanding process as a specification of those facts about the structure of a sentence which are required for a potential sequence of elaborative and interpretive steps (which may or may not take place, as occasion demands or as information in a subsequent input provides for).

What is offered, then, is a rather limited version of sentence understanding. This limitation is not just strategic, but, I believe, substantive. There may be little to be said for any notion of sentence recognition which goes much beyond this limited characterization. More detailed analyses may involve processes which are not language specific and hence properly construed as part of a more general model of cognitive functions (e.g., problem solving, inference, etc.).

II. EXPERIMENTAL ISSUES

The preceding discussion suggests some of the kinds of facts about sentences which listeners must establish in order to provide an interpretation of them. However, given some set of structural facts which are crucial to the interpretation of sentences, we must then ask, more precisely, how listeners extract those structural facts from the information which is present in speech signals.

There are two major lines of attack on the question of how listeners assign structural analyses to sentences. One is by attempting to specify in detail computational routines which will take the information represented in a string of lexical items and yield a syntactic description of the string; the other is experimental investigation of sentence comprehension in order to establish a set of constraints on the character of information processing routines which perform the desired transduction. It is the latter of these approaches that we will address here.

Two experimental issues are of special interest: these are the perceptual segmentation of sentences and the perceptual complexity of sentences.

The interest of the segmentation problem is self-evident. One wants to know the processes by which the speech signal is decoded into its component lexical items, and moreover, to know what are the limits on the number of items over which structural inferences are normally integrated. As George Miller (1962) pointed out so cogently several years ago, it is obvious that decisions about the structure of the speech signal cannot be made at the same rate as phonetic information is normally presented to the system. Some process for making simultaneous decisions about relatively large sequences of the speech signal is necessary. Decisions are evidently not made about each sound unit as it occurs; at the very least, words or short sequences of words must be in some sense primary units of analysis in the perceptual system. Some of the research mentioned below is aimed at making a somewhat more precise statement about the nature of such decision units or perceptual segments.

The complexity issue is somewhat different. We would like to make valid inferences about the character of the systems which assign structure to sentences. But it is very hard to establish constraints on the kinds of systems which one proposes for such a psychological process. One very powerful one, of course, is that the system assign the correct structures to the strings under analysis, but there are a large number of ways of accomplishing that end. One would like to find the process corresponding to that employed by human speaker/hearers. The study of complexity is in aid of establishing constraints on theory building in this area. Thus, we are interested in comprehension errors and more generally in whatever factors contribute to comprehension difficulty even when no overt error results. On the one hand, if we can order sentences by their perceptual difficulty, an examination of their structural properties may suggest something of the way in which structural assignment is accomplished. On the other hand, we will require of our perceptual model that, so long as it successfully assigns structural descriptions to strings, the operations by which it does so must provide in a natural way for comprehension errors and for the obtained complexity ordering for sentences. In particular, we would expect that the greater the number of processing operations requir-ed by the perceptual device in order to assign a structural description to a string, the more perceptually complex the string should be. This is an assumption fraught with difficulties which I will forebear to enumerate here. It is sufficient to say that there are problems in mapping a complexity ordering onto models of the process of understanding a sentence; it is by no means a simple or conclusive step. In spite of these difficulties, com-plexity experiments seem to be one of the most direct ways of providing experimentally established constraints on theories of sentence perception.

It is evident that these two foci of research do not define mutually exclusive sets of experimental problems. Nonetheless, they have tended to encourage an interest in different parameters of the comprehension process. Typically, segmentation studies have involved features of the surface analysis of sentences (e.g., Garrett et al., 1966; Wingfield and Klein, 1971; Holmes and Forster, 1970; Martin and Strange, 1968, et al.), while complexity studies have revolved more directly about features of the underlying structure of sentences and its transformational relation to their surface form (Miller and McKean, 1964; Compton, 1967; Fodor et al., 1968; Hakes, 1972; Forster, 1970).

III. THE RELATION OF COMPLEXITY AND SEGMENTATION

There is a more interesting way to think about the relation between these two research concerns than the straightforward observation that segmentation errors or difficulties may increase comprehension difficulty. The interaction of complexity and segmentation variables may be thought of in terms of hypotheses about the order of sentence processing events. We described complexity above as a consequence of the number of decisions that must be made in processing a sentence. That, of course, is too simple; it is not just the number of decisions that must be taken account of, but the rate at which decisions must be made. Alternatively, it is a question of *where* decisions are made in the course of sentence processing. Two sentences which require the same number of computational steps for the assignment of structure may, nevertheless, differ in their perceptual difficulty. A sentence which requires decision making to be postponed until the sentence has been substantially received may be more difficult than a sentence which distributes information sufficient to support structural decisions throughout the string. (For example, in a doubly self-embedded sentence, major structural decisions must be postponed until almost the end of the string.)

It is assumed that conditions which require delay in decision making may result in an increase in the difficulty of understanding a sentence. On the other hand, in some cases the delay of decision may *reduce* complexity. Miller's argument in 'Decision Units in the Perception of speech' (1962) is based on the observation that simultaneous decisions about a number of speech sounds may be simpler to make than a series of decisions about speech sounds taken individually.

This suggests a complex trade-off relation between delay in decision making, number of computational decisions required, and the character of the structural decision being made. The efficiency of making simultaneous decisions over a relatively long stretch of speech must be balanced against the limits on short-term memory (as well as against possible limits on the number of simultaneous decisions that can be made). Thus, minimizing computational difficulty requires the sentence processing system to find decision-making points (1) which will not exceed short-term memory requirements, (2) at which sufficient information to support decisions is likely to have been received, and (3) at which decisions made on current portions of the string will interact minimally with analysis of subsequent portions. In short, subject to the limitations of short-term memory, one wants to be able to make structural decisions that antecedent context will support and that posterior context will not invalidate.

Such considerations inspire a view of the comprehension process as one in which a substring of several elements is first isolated and then evaluated for its structural and interpretive consequences. This contrasts with a view in which each successive element of the string is immediately assigned a role in whatever structure is determined by antecedent context, and that element in turn establishes a range of structural options for the next element presented (see, e.g., Martin and Roberts, 1966; or Hockett, 1961). There is not presently a conclusive empirical resolution of this matter, but there are a variety of experimental results which bear on it. I will discuss some of those experiments in terms of the following three working hypotheses:

(1) Surface clause boundaries isolate the major perceptual processing units of sentences.

(2) Detailed surface constituency is a relatively 'late' consequence of sentence analysis: in particular, any non-clausal substring which is a constituent is elaborated after the right-hand boundary of the clause containing it.

(3) Word boundaries are an exception to (2); their assignment may not be held in abeyance until the occurrence of decisive posterior context.

A. *The Perceptual Effects of Constituent Structure: Clause Boundaries*

For several years a number of my colleagues and I have been using a particular experimental technique to explore the problem of segmentation of speech. Briefly, the experimental technique consists of placing a very short burst of noise (a 'click' of 30–40 ms duration) in sentences and requesting listeners to locate the click relative to the sentence. Typically, sentence and click are presented dichotically. For example, in his right ear, a subject might hear the sentence, 'John's youngest daugther wears hair in a bizarre fashion', while in his left ear he will hear a click sometime during the course of the sentence. Immediately following the presentation of the stimuli, the subject must indicate his judgment of the click location (i.e., by noting which word or speech sound the click occurred in or adjacent to).

We have interpreted the accuracy of location and the distribution of errors for clocks objectively placed at various points in sentences as indicative of their perceptual segmentation. Much of our early research effort was aimed at showing a correlation between distribution of click location errors and the constituent structure of sentences, and further, that such errors occur *during and as a consequence* of the perceptual processing of sentences. The correlation between click location and constituent structure has been found by several different investigators in laboratories from Melbourne (Holmes and Forster, 1970) to Champaign-Urbana (Berry, 1970), among others. The claim that sentence processing is the source of location errors is, of course, more difficult to establish conclusively. The results so far seem to indicate that gross memory effects, rehearsal strategies, acoustic correlates of prosodic features and response biases are not the primary determinants of the relation between click location errors and syntax. (For a review of some click research studies see Garrett and Bever, 1974.) Though research continues on this question, we have also been pursuing research which assumes the validity of a sentence processing interpretation of click location.

In particular, we have asked the question: Is the location of clicks responsive to all constituent structure boundaries, or is it responsive only to certain varieties of boundaries? In our initial thinking about the problem we assumed that the degree of effect on click location could be predicted by the number of constituents that a click interrupted at any point in a sentence; i.e., that every constituent contributed in some measure to the effect. Very early on, however, various irregularities in our experimental results led us to consider seriously the possibility that certain constituent structure boundaries were more effective than others in producing click location errors. We made two approaches to this question: (1) a concerted effort to evaluate effects of minor constituent structure boundaries and (2) an attempt to contrast the effects of boundaries for structures that were immediately dominated by a sentence node (e.g., relative clauses or complement sentences) with the effects of constituent boundaries for structures not so dominated. These research efforts indicate little effect of minor constituent structure and have provided strong support for the view that the presence of an embedded sentence is an important determinant of click location errors (see Bever *et al.*, 1966; Bever *et al.*, 1969; Garrett and Bever, 1974). Whether the increased effect for boundaries of embedded sentences holds only for surface clauses or for the boundary between any two words assigned to different sentoids (underlying sentences) remains at present a vexed issue (cf. Chapin *et al.*, 1972).

However, the perceptual salience of clausal boundaries does not depend solely on results like the preceding. Caplan (1972) found that the latency for indicating the presence of a given word in a sentence was affected by clausal boundaries. He contrasted latencies for sentence pairs such as (a) and (b) below, in which the subject's task was to press a reaction time key indicating 'yes'/or 'no' when presented with a single word at the end of the sentence; e.g.,

(a)   Now that artists are working in oil, prints are rare. (50 ms. pure tone) *oil*

(b)   Now that artists aren't working, oil prints are rare. (50 ms. pure tone) *oil*

Note that the interval from presentation of the *target* item and the *probe* at sentences end (i.e. the word 'oil') is the same for both (a) and (b); this was insured by making the lexical sequence starting at the word 'oil' acoustically identical (by tape slicing) in the two versions. Nonetheless, latencies for sentences like (a) were significantly greater than for sentences like (b). When the probe target was for a word in the last clause heard, subjects could respond more quickly than if the target word was part of the preceding clause. We have twice successfully replicated this effect with various controls for aspects of structure that were partially correlated with the clausal variable. In general, when a clause boundary intervenes between probe presentation and target occurrence, reaction time is elevated. We interpret this as an indication that each clause is a unit in the processing routine for the sentence, and that whether an item is in the processing system or in short-term memory depends on whether clausal structure has been assigned or not.

In the introductory remarks it was suggested that considerations of computational efficiency would seem to dictate a delay in some processing decisions. Clauses appear to be the most natural candidate for the domain of such delay strategies, and thus the boundaries of clauses would be expected to show processing 'discontinuities' if there is anything to these speculations. The results of the click location and the probe latency studies do provide empirical support for the perceptual significance of such boundaries, but they do not afford direct experimental support for the more specific claim that occurrence of a clause boundary precipitates delayed decisions about sentence structure. Studies of the perceptual effects of ambiguity, however, provide some relevant results.

If one were looking for a likely source of computational difficulty in the understanding of sentences, ambiguity is among the first candidates one would consider. The presence of an ambiguity is, by definition, the presence of a computational option in the analysis of a sentence. If deciding among possible analyses of a string is a source of computational difficulty, ambiguity should contribute to the difficulty of understanding a sentence. N.B.: this need not be consciously perceived ambiguity; though ambiguity is extremely common in the speech we hear, it is extremely *un*common for such ambiguity to be noticed in normal conversation. It is only when the *wrong* structural option – given the context of a discourse – has been chosen that ambiguities are ordinarily remarked on (i.e., 'garden-path' cases).[1] Thus, there is a *prima facie* case for the view that some method for coping with the presence of ambiguities is a part of our normal computational scheme for sentences. (By 'coping' I mean avoiding the consequences of selecting the wrong computational option.)

The outcome of experimental studies of ambiguity has been varied. Some studies appear to show that ambiguities have an effect only in cases in which the situationally wrong computational option is picked, while others appear to show that the mere presence of an ambiguity increases comprehension difficulty even when the situationally correct interpretation is chosen. (See Garrett, 1970 for a review.) The interesting feature for our discussion is that these two classes of studies can also be distinguished by the point at which measures of comprehension were taken. In studies which show *no* effect (except for 'garden-path' cases) of ambiguity, the measures of difficulty were taken after the completion of the stimulus sentence. In studies which do show an effect of ambiguity, measures of comprehension difficulty were taken during the presentation of the stimulus sentences. The inference is obvious: The increase in computational load associated with an ambiguity is restricted to the point in time at which the computational options have not been decided among. Our earlier discussion would suggest that the latest point at which computational options remain open is the end of the clause in which an ambiguity occurs. Measures taken after that point should show only 'garden path' effects.

Bever, Hurtig and I have done an experiment focussed on this question.

We used a paradigm similar to one from earlier work by MacKay (1966). In this experimental situation subjects are presented with a sentence fragment and required to provide a grammatical and sensible completion for it. The dependent measure is time taken to begin a completion. Response times for sentence fragements containing an ambiguity are compared with those for fragments with no ambiguities present. The ambiguous and unambiguous fragments are kept as nearly the same as possible.

MacKay found that ambiguous fragments were significantly more difficult to provide completions for than were their unambiguous counterparts. The effects, however, were somewhat erratic. If his data are re-examined for possible effects of clausal structure, an interesting finding emerges: MacKay's stimulus fragments can be categorized as ending at a possible clause boundary ('After taking the right turn, ...'), or internal to a constituent ('Although the solution seemed clear in ...'). The primary source of difference between ambiguous and unambiguous fragments in his data derived from stimuli of the latter sort – the incomplete constituents.

In our own experiment (Bever *et al.*, 1973) we specifically manipulated this variable with matched sets of stimulus fragments (e.g., ambiguous complete: 'although the solution seemed clear in class, ...'; *un*ambiguous complete: 'although the answer seemed clear in class, ...'; ambiguous incomplete: 'although the answer seemed clear in, ..., etc.). We tested three types of ambiguity (lexical, bracketing, and deep structure); we found a significant effect only for deep structure ambiguities. The lack of effect for lexical and bracketing cases dictates caution (although there is some reason to expect a lesser effect of such ambiguities), but the deep structure effects were quite striking. When a fragment ended in an incomplete constituent, there was significantly greater difficulty in completing the ambiguous version, but when the fragment ended at a potential clause boundary there is no hint of such a difference (if anything the relation is reversed).[2] Thus, it appears that when there is evidence in the stimulus string that a clause boundary has been reached, subjects may close their structural options; when the clause is not completed, structural options remain open long enough to interfere with the efficiency of the sentence completion operation.

This result, when considered with the pattern of results from other ambiguity studies and the click and probe studies, lends support to the view that ends of clauses are points at which structural decisions are made and that this is done regardless of whether the information in the clause is completely sufficient to support unambiguously a given interpretation. The material in the section below can also be seen as complementary to the findings we have just been discussing.

B. *Surface Structure is a Late Consequence of Sentence Processing*

From the results that 'major' constituent boundaries (i.e., S-dominated surface constituents) have an important effect on click location errors while 'minor' constituent boundaries (e.g., the boundary between a verb and its object noun phrase) have a miniscule effect if any, one could derive two conclusions. The first of these is that the click location paradigm is simply insensitive to minor constituent structure and reveals only the grosser aspects of the processing of sentences. However, a second possible conclusion is that click location is indeed sensitive to *all* of the constituent structure that is present at the point in sentence processing where the click location judgment is normally made, but that minor constituent structure boundaries have not yet been developed at that point.

Fodor and I have tried to find an experimental test of this latter view. We wanted to ask whether click location errors are sensitive to minor constituent boundaries under conditions where we believe such boundaries should have been developed. We assumed that if a listener is given more than the usual amount of time to consider a sentence, a more detailed analysis will be available to him. The logic of the argument is then straightforward. If under such circumstances clicks *are* affected by minor constituent boundaries, then the *failure* of such boundaries to show an effect in past experiments may plausibly be interpreted as evidence that minor constituent structure is developed relatively late in the processing routine.

The experiment is a difficult one to perform. If one gives additional computational time, one must at the same time postpone the occasion for a click location error. That is, one wishes the occurrence of the error to be displaced in time to the point at which minor constituent structure is built up. We have employed the following paradigm. Subjects in one group were given two immediately successive presentations of the same sentence. The first occurrence of the sentence does *not* contain a click; the second occurrence does. Location errors in this condition were compared with those for another group which received only a single presentation of the sentence containing a click. The initial presentation of the sentence with *no* click is assumed to provide the listener with the basis for a more fine-grained analysis of the sentence on its second presentation. If the click location errors are sensitive to whatever constituent boundaries are present, effects of minor constituent boundaries should increase under these conditions.

Experiments we have done so far (Fodor and Garrett, 1971) do show the expected effect for non-clasusal subject-predicate boundaries. Their effects on click location are significantly enhanced by double presentation in groups where *clausal* effects are *not* enhanced. Present results for verb/ object breaks and prepositional phrase boundaries are less clear, although they are in the expected direction. Further research is in progress, but at the present moment we believe that the research supports the view that assignment of minor constituent boundaries is a relatively late operation in the processing of sentences.

An experiment by Bever (personal communication) gives further support for this view. When subjects had to delay their report of click location for an interval of 10 s following stimulus presentation, Bever found a significant increase in the effects of minor constituent boundaries on location errors. This is the result one would expect if minor constituent structure requires more time for its elaboration than does major constituent structure.

Notice that this view, if it can be maintained, has the very interesting consequence that the inference of underlying grammatical relations for sentences cannot be the consequence of the development of a lowest level, detailed constituent structure for the string. Rather the inference of underlying structure relations proceeds in the absence of such an analysis. This further suggests that on-line computational difficulty of a sentence may be affected primarily by the step to underlying grammatical functions and not by the determination of detailed bracketing of the surface structure.

C. Word Segmentation Can't Wait

The last of the three working hypotheses is one for which there is little experimental evidence, but it is the one about which I am most confident. The claim is simply that word level segmentation of an input string happens very early in the processing sequence and, while subject to contextual influences, such segmentation does not ordinarily await the appearence of decisive posterior contexts.

It is suggested in the preceding section that decisions about details of constituent structure may be delayed until clause boundaries. This delay can be understood as one which maximizes the potential support for a structural inference; such a structural decision may, within limits, be postponed in the interests of possibly relevant posterior information. It seems unlikely that the same is true of word level segmentation, however; particular lexical items provide most of the 'raw material' for subsequent interpretive operations.

One experiment (Garrett, 1965) that bears on this claim suggests that prior context can indeed significantly influence decisions about word segmentation, but that posterior context does not.

The experiment is a click experiment, and it is rather complicated. The principal objects of interest in this experiment are what might be called 'phonetic' ambiguities. These are sound sequences with an interpretation in which the entire sequence is a single word, and an interpretation in which the sequence is divided into two or more words. Thus the contrast is between the presence or absence of a word boundary in a phonetic string. The matter of which interpretation (and thus the presence or absence of a word boundary) was operative in any given presentation was determined by a context phrase. The sentences were so constructed that this context phrase could appear either prior to or following the occurrence of the ambiguous phonetic sequence. The effect of the context was to 'disambiguate' the phonetic string: thus there were cases of both 'pre-disambiguation' and 'post-disambiguation'. For example, one of the stimulus pairs was the following:

(a) Before making any long distance phone calls John inquired about both the day rates and the /najtrejts/[3] in order to be sure not to waste money'. (word boundary present; pre-disambiguation).

(b) Before making any mining commitments John inquired about both the bauxites and the /najtrejts/[4] in order to be sure not to waste money', (no word boundary; pre-disambiguation).

The post-disambiguation versions of these two were produced by exhanging the introductory and final clauses and by moving the words 'day rates' and 'bauxites' to positions following the tested phonetic string.

Three such sets of 4 stimulus strings were prepared (for three different phonetic ambiguities). The phonetically ambiguous sequences in the stimulus sentences were all acoustically indentical. (This was accomplished by cross-recording and tape splicing.)

The response measure for this experiment was the frequency with which listeners judged the position of clicks in two successively presented versions of the sentence as being the same. Every such judgment was an error since clicks were placed *at* the *potential* word boundary (i.e., internal to the sequence) for the first presentation and at the *end* of the phonetic ambiguity for the second presentation. On the assumption that clicks tend to be displaced from within perceptual units. and assuming that words *are* units of perceptual analysis, more 'same' judgments should be produced for sentence versions with *no* word boundary internal to the phonetic sequence (e.g., example (b) above).

Given these assumptions, we ask two questions: Was the assignment of word boundaries affected by sentence context, and was there a difference in the effect of prior and posterior contexts?

If context does influence the assignment of word boundaries, and equally so for prior and posterior context, the results would tell us little about the point at which word boundaries are assigned. The results showed, however, that prior contexts did affect the assignment of word boundaries, but the posterior context did not. For example, in the 'night rate' and 'nitrate' contrast, for the pre-disambiguation condition, the version with a word boundary at the click location ('night rate') had approximately half as many errors ('same' judgments) as the version ('nitrate') which does not have a word boundary at the click position. This pattern held for two of the three different phonetic cases and each was significant ($p < 0.01$). The third case showed no significant variance across conditions. This indicates, not too surprisingly, that context can introduce a word boundary into a phonetically ambiguous sequence.

The comparison of pre- and post-disambiguated versions leads to a more interesting conclusion, however. The posterior context condition did *not* show a significant difference between sentence versions with word boundaries and those without word boundaries. The error rate for the two interpretations was almost identical in all cases. This supports the claim that word segmentation does not wait on posterior context (at least not for the interval required in these sentences – about 4 syllables).

If perceptual segmentation could be delayed till posterior context, both pre- and post-disambiguation context should have been successful in producing a difference between the word boundary conditions. They were not.

There is a further, somewhat risky inference one can make from these results: that the segmentation strategy is a maximizing strategy; that is, word boundaries are inserted only where there is contextual or acoustic information which demands that a boundary be inserted; as *few* boundaries as are compatible with the input are inserted rather than as many as are compatible. The admittedly weak support for this claim in the present experiment is that the error rate for pre-disambiguation versions *without* a word boundary and the error rates for post-disambiguated versions with and without word boundaries are virtually indentical in all the experimental conditions. (The pattern of results for a minimizing strategy would have been for the two post-disambiguation conditions to have the same error rate as the pre-disambiguation condition *with* a word boundary – i.e., a low error rate. One might then speak of 'boundary excision' rather than 'boundary insertion'.)

Thus, these data give some support for the view that word level segmentation is not entirely determined by acoustic properties of the string – context can influence word level segmentation. But beyond that, it appears that the decision about word boundaries is not one that is delayed until all of the contextual material relevant to the decision has been received.

These results and those discussed under our other two working hypotheses would suggest that the initial perceptual segmentation of a sentence reflects its word and clausal structure but not other details of its derived constitutent structure. Further, we have discussed some evidence that clausal boundaries are points at which delayed decisions about sentence structure are made. While such interpretations are somewhat speculative given the complexity of the system we are seeking to explain, they should illustrate the possibility of an experimental resolution of even quite detailed questions about sentence processing activities.

Dept. of Psychology,
Massachusetts Institute of Technology,
Cambridge, Mass., U.S.A.

NOTES

* This work was supported in part by NIMH Grant No. HD 05168-02 to Professors J. A. Fodor and M. F. Garrett.

[1] Sentences which mislead listeners (either by context or by common assumption) are often referred to as 'garden-path' sentences; I will use the term to refer to circumstances in which the initially selected interpretation for a word or phrase is disconfirmed for the listener by subsequent context.

[2] The reversal of effects for ambiguous and unambiguous fragments in the complete constituent condition suggests, along with some other evidence, that there may be parallel processing of alternative readings of sentences or portions of sentences. However, the evidence is at present too weak to present more than a very interesting possibility for future research.

[3] i.e. 'night rates'.

[4] i.e. 'nitrates'.

BIBLIOGRAPHY

Berry, R., 'A Critical Review of Noise Location during Simultaneously Presented Sentences', unpublished Ph.D. dissertation, University of Illinois, 1970.

Bever, T., Fodor, J., and Garrett, M., 'Speech Perception: Some Experimental Results for Sentences', Invited Paper at the *International Congress of Psychology*, Moscow, U.S.S.R., 1966.

Bever, T. G., Garrett, M., and Hurtig, R., 'The Interaction of Perceptual Processes and Ambiguous Sentences', accepted for publication in *Memory and Cognition* (to appear in 1973).

Bever, T. G., Lackner, J. R., and Kirk, R., 'The Underlying Structures of Sentences are the Primary Units of Immediate Speech Processing', *Perception and Psychophysics* 5 (1969) 225-231.

Caplan, D., 'Clause Boundaries and Recognition Latencies for Words in Sentences, *Perception and Psychophysics* 12 (1972) 73-76.

Chapin, P., Smith, T., and Abrahamson, A., 'Two Factors in Perceptual Segmentation of Speech', *Journal of Verbal Learning and Verbal Behavior* 11 (1972) 164-173.

Compton, A., 'Aural Perception of Different Syntactic Structures and Lengths', *Language and Speech* 10 (1967) 81-87.

Fodor, J. A. and Garrett, M., 'A Consolidation Effect in Sentence Perception', *Quarterly Progress Report of the Research Laboratory of Electronics*, No. 100, MIT, 1971.

Fodor, J., Garrett, M., and Bever, T. G., 'Some Syntactic Determinants of Sentential Complexity. II: Verb Structure', *Perception and Psychophysics* 3 (1968) 453-461.

Forster, K. I., 'Visual Perception of Rapidly Presented Word Sequences of Varying Complexity', *Perception and Psychophysics* 8 (1970) 215-221.

Garrett, M., 'Syntactic Structures and Judgments of Auditory Events: A Study of the Perception of Extraneous Noise in Sentences', unpublished Ph.D. dissertation, University of Illinois, 1965.

Garrett, M., 'Does Ambiguity Complicate the Perception of Sentences?', in *Advances in Psycholinguistics* (ed. by G. Flores d'Arcais and W. Levelt), North-Holland Co., Amsterdam, 1970.

Garrett, M. and Bever, T. G., 'The Perceptual Segmentation of Sentences', in *The Structure and Psychology of Language* (ed. by T. Bever and W. Weksel), Mouton and Co., The Hague (in press).

114   MERRILL GARRETT

Garrett, M., Bever, T. and Fodor, J., 'The Active Use of Grammar in Speech Perception', *Perception and Psychophysics* 1 (1966) 30–32.
Hakes, D., 'Effects of Reducing Complement Constructions on Sentence Comprehension', *Journal of Verbal Learning and Verbal Behavior* 11 (1972) 278–286.
Hockett, C., 'Grammar for the Hearer', in R. Jakobson (ed.), *Structure of Language and Its Mathematical Aspects; Proceedings of the Twelfth Symposium in Applied Mathematics* 12, Amer. Math. Soc., 1961.
Holmes, V. M. and Forster, K. I., 'Detection of Extraneous Signals During Sentence Recognition', *Perception and Psychophysics* 7 (1970) 297–301.
Martin, K. and Roberts, E., 'Grammatical Factors in Sentence Retention', *J. of Verbal Learning and Verbal Behavior* 5 (1966) 211–218.
Martin, J. G. and Strange, W., 'The Perception of Hesitation in Spontaneous Speech', *Perception and Psychophysics* 3, (1968) 427–438(b).
Miller, G., 'Decision Units in the Perception of Speech', *Int. Radio Eng. Transactions on Information Theory* IT-8 (1962) 81–83.
Miller, G. and McKean, K., 'A Chronometric Study of Some Relations between Sentences', *Quarterly Journal of Experimental Psychology* 16 (1964) 297–308.
Wingfield, A. and Klein, J. F., 'Syntactic Structure and Acoustic Pattern in Speech Perception', *Perception and Psychophysics* 9 (1971) 23–25.

KENNETH I. FORSTER

LINGUISTIC STRUCTURE AND SENTENCE PRODUCTION*

It is generally accepted that a careful distinction must be drawn between theories of a language user's competence and theories of a language user's performance. The former theories describe what the user knows about the sentence of his language, whereas the latter theories describe how this knowledge is put to use in the task of producing or understanding particular sentences. This paper is concerned with problems involved in the second type of theory, and in particular, with the task of providing a model of the control system involved in sentence production. The total sequence of operations involved in the production of a sentence is assumed to be analyzable into at least three components: (a) the class of operations involved in determining the content of the message to be encoded, (b) the class of operations involved in converting the message to a sequence of morphemes, and (c) the class of operations involved in converting this morpheme sequence into the appropriate commands to the articulatory system. Only the second of these three components will be considered in this paper.

It should be pointed out immediately that no detailed model of sentence production has yet been proposed – nor will such a model be proposed here. At most, all that can be hoped for is a set of empirical results that bear on the problem. Such results are not easily obtained. For example, conventional experimental techniques, such as the observation of correlations between experimenter controlled inputs and response outputs, are out of the question, since the inputs to the sentence producer are not understood, and certainly cannot be controlled experimentally.[1] Consequently, experimenters in the field have typically resorted to relatively indirect methods. For example, experimental techniques may be abandoned, and the data collected by means of naturalistic observation. Maclay and Osgood (1959) have adopted this approach in their analysis of hesitations and errors in naturally occurring utterances. If experimental methods are used, the investigators are typically forced to study such variables as the difficulty involved in learning and recalling different

C. Cherry (ed.), Pragmatic Aspects of Human Communication, 115–143. *All Rights Reserved*
Copyright © 1974 *by D. Reidel Publishing Company, Dordrecht-Holland*

types of sentences (Johnson, 1965; Mehler, 1963). It goes without saying that the task of learning a sentence is not the same as the task of producing (or understanding) a sentence, although the former task may certainly include the latter. Since it appears that any approach to sentence production is necessarily relatively indirect, it becomes essential to attack the problem on as wide a methodological front as possible. Thus, the purpose of the present paper is to outline a different, but equally indirect approach, together with some preliminary results.

It has been pointed out that it is difficult to place constraints on the input to the sentence producer. Is it likely that any useful purpose would be served by placing instead constraints on the *output* of this system? For example, an experiment could be conducted in which the subjects are required to construct as quickly as possible a sentence of eight words in length, the second word being *after*. Such an experiment will be useful (i.e., informative) only if it is possible to establish a meaningful relationship between the nature of the constraint and some aspect of the subject's performance (such as the time required to produce a sentence meeting these constraints). Many methods of arranging constraints will probably prove to be relatively uninformative. For example, Guilford (1959) includes a task of this nature in an intelligence test battery. In this case, the subject is required to construct a sentence, the first word beginning with the letter *t*, the second with *h*, the third with *d*, etc. This task serves the intelligence tester's purpose, since presumably the more rapidly the subject can identify suitable sentences (relative to other subjects), the greater his verbal fluency. But this technique is not likely to reveal any properties of the process by which the subject arrives at a solution. If a given item in the test is difficult to solve, the only inference to be made is that there are relatively few sentences meeting the constraints specified. Thus, a given item would remain constant in difficulty relative to other items, no matter what procedure was used to reach a solution.

Consider a different approach. Instead of specifying the initial letters of each word, we specify that the sentence should contain certain words. We may, for example, specify that the sentence should begin with a particular sequence of words, or alternatively, that it should end with a particular sequence. If these types of items are compared, we can ask whether specifying the end of the sentence would make the task more difficult than specifying the beginning. For the moment, assume that if a large number of items of each type is used, then, on the average, the number of solutions is constant for each task. Any observed difference in the difficulty of the two tasks would then presumably be a function of the method used by subjects to arrive at a solution. If it is further assumed that, in general, the only relevant abilities possessed by the subject are those normally used for sentence production and understanding, then some information about these abilities should be provided by the experiment.

This particular method of devising constraints appears to be relevant to the proposal that sentence production is, in some sense, a 'left to right' process. This proposal, first formulated by Yngve (1960, 1961), asserts generally that the speaker attempts to plan in detail the structure of only those segments of the sentence which immediately require utterance. Thus the speaker plans in detail the structure of the beginning of the sentence before the middle, and plans in detail the middle of the sentence before the end. If this view is correct, then it seems reasonable to suggest that speakers will be accustomed to planning the end of the sentence, given that they are already committed to the beginning of the sentence (by virtue of having already spoken it). Conversely, speakers should be relatively unaccustomed to planning the beginning of the sentence, given that they are already committed to the end of the sentence. In the normal speech situation, the notion of commitment implies that the speaker himself has already made decisions about the form of a particular segment. When this situation is translated into the terms of the experiment proposed above, the notion of commitment implies that the *experimenter* has already made decisions (which the subject must accept as binding) about the particular segment of the sentence. If there is any parallel between the experimental situation and the normal speech situation, then it should be the case that subjects will experience more difficulty in producing a sentence when the end has been specified in advance, than when the beginning has been specified in advance.

This hypothesis was first tested (Forster, 1964) in the following way. Generally, the subjects of the experiment were given a number of both types of items, and were told to complete them as quickly as possible. The difficulty of each type of item can be determined either by measuring how long the subjects take to complete each item (in which case, the test must be administered to single subjects), or by determining how many items of a given type can be completed in a fixed period of time (in which case, the test may be administered simultaneously to a large number of subjects). The latter procedure, being more economical, was adopted, and the subjects were given blocks of items (five items of one type in each block), each to be completed within 75 seconds.

The items themselves were constructed in the following way. Forty English sentences, each having an even number of words, and each between 10 and 16 words in length, were selected from novels, magazines, etc. Each sentence was then divided at the midpoint, producing two segments equal in length. An item in which the end (or second half) of the sentence has been specified in advance is constructed by simply deleting the first half of the sentence. Such an item will be referred to as a *left-deleted* (LD) item. In order to construct an item in which the beginning of the sentence has been specified in advance, the second half of the sentence is deleted. This type of item will be referred to as a *right-deleted* (RD) item. In each case, each deleted word was replaced by a blank, and the subjects were constrained to provide the same number of words in their completion as there were blanks. Thus the originally selected sentence *On his return to the house he found the woman in a state of great agitation* yielded the following items:

(1)   LD: .... the woman in a state of great agitation.
(2)   RD: On his return to the house he found ....

The subjects were given an alternating sequence of blocks of RD and LD items, until a total of four blocks of each type had been presented. The responses were scored such that each perfectly acceptable sentence produced by the subject received a score of 2, each ungrammatical, or semantically anomalous sentence received a score of 0, with a score of 1 reserved for borderline cases (typically used in less than 5% of cases).

The results of this experiment were clear-cut. Of the sixty college students serving as subjects, only two obtained a higher score for LD items than for RD items. Over all subjects, the mean score per block (total possible being 10) of RD items was 5.49 as opposed to a mean score of 3.27 for LD items. The probability that this difference is due to chance is less than 0.001.

Before these results can be taken as support of the proposed hypothesis, certain conditions must be satisfied. For example, it is possible that in constructing the test, the decision as to whether a given sentence should produce an LD or an RD item was made in such a way that the more complex sentences were consistently chosen to yield LD items. But this cannot be so, since each sentence generated both an LD and an RD item – half of the subjects receiving the LD version, and half the RD version. A different problem involves the already mentioned assumption that the number of possible completions is constant for both types of items. Let the set of all possible completions of a given item be termed the *completion set*. Since the completions are constrained with respect to length, the completion set of any item will contain finitely many members. However, if the completion sets for LD items tended to be smaller than the completion sets for RD items, the results of the experiment could be shown to be a function of a property of the language itself, rather than a function of the methods used by subjects to identify solutions. In support of this argument, we can point to items where the LD completion set is indeed smaller, as evidenced by comparison of items (3) and (4) below, which were both derived from the same sentence:

(3)   .... the old man come running through the forest.

(4)   The young boy was very surprised to see ....

In (3) the subject is limited in the choice of the verb to constructions such as *saw, noticed, perceived, felt*, etc. But in (4), no such narrow restriction is placed on the subject. However, it is also possible to point to examples, such as (5) and (6) below, in which exactly the reverse situation appears to be the case:

(5)   ...... wife nor his child would return.

(6)   He remarked pitifully that neither his ......

The completion of (6) here is virtually restricted to the form *NP–nor–NP–VP*, whereas in (5) more freedom is provided, the only rigid constraint being the required use of *neither*.

The only convincing solution to this problem would involve an enumeration of the members of the completion sets. Since this is not feasible, we must resort to the following arguments. First, it seems implausible that the grammar of English is such that the number of different ways of specifying the second half of a sentence tends to be greater than the number of ways of specifying the first half. Second, if such a view were correct, then one would expect that the probability of two or more subjects selecting the same completion would be higher in the case of LD items than in the case of RD items. In fact, examination of a sample of completions shows precisely the reverse trend. If we consider the completions as sequences of word-types, then the probability of a subject selecting the same sequence of word-types as in the original sentence from which the item was derived, was slightly higher in the case of RD items. This suggests that, if anything, the effective RD completion set tends to be smaller than the effective LD completion set.

A further problem involves the constraint on the length of the completion. This was originally introduced to control the time required to actually write the completion. However, it is entirely possible that if subjects were permitted to produce completions of any desired length, the difference between RD and LD items may well disappear. The results of such an experiment are available (Forster, 1966b). The conditions of this experiment duplicated those of the first, except that subjects were free to provide completions of any length. Since this task was markedly easier than the first, the time allowed for each block of items was reduced to 18 seconds. Under these conditions, the mean score per block of RD items was 5.42, as opposed to a mean score of 4.03 for LD items, this difference being statistically significant. Although the RD–LD difference is found, its magnitude is diminished. This is not surprising, since the task as a whole is easier.

Returning to the analysis of the first experiment, it was suggested that the RD–LD difference was not due to variation in the size of the completion sets. But if we consider one RD item with a larger completion set than another RD item, it ought to be the case that the former item is easier to complete than the latter. The same ought to be true of LD items. To put the point more precisely, although variation in completion set size may not account for variance in difficulty between deletion types, it may still account for variance within deletion types. In order to assess this hypothesis, we must once again consider the problem of estimating the size of completion sets. Presumably, there are two factors responsible for limiting the size of the completion set. First, the subjects must ensure that the completion, when attached to the presented string (the sequence of words presented to the subject for completion), does not violate semantic requirements. Second, he must ensure that the completion does not violate syntactic requirements. Of these two factors, the second probably has the greatest effect. If, in some way, the extent of the semantic and syntactic constraints placed on the completion by the presented string could be assessed, then one would have at least an estimate of the size of the completion set. No simple method of accomplishing this result for the operation of semantic factors is available, but the following method appears to achieve plausible results for the operation of syntactic factors.

Consider the original sentence from which any particular item is derived. The surface structure of this sentence can be represented as a hierarchical arrangement of constituents. If we consider the location of the cutting point dividing the sentence into two equal segments, it will be noticed that this cutting point lies within the boundaries of some constituents, but not others. Thus, when either the first or second half of the sentence is deleted, some constituents are left intact, while others are damaged or eliminated altogether. But if part of a constituent has been removed, the subject is forced to reconstruct that constituent, perhaps changing it completely, but nevertheless restoring a full constituent. It is assumed that the greater the number of constituents requiring restoration, the more constraints are placed upon the completion, and the smaller becomes the completion set.

An example should serve to make the argument clearer. In (7), below, the constituents of a sentence are indicated in terms of a bracketing notation:

(7)   ((After((being released)(on bail)))(she(brooded(over(her arrest))))).

Thus, according to this analysis, the constituents of the sentence are: *being released, on bail, being released on bail, after being released on bail, her arrest, over her arrest,* etc. If the cutting point is located (as it was in the experiment) between *bail* and *she*, only one constituent (the sentence itself) is damaged when either the first or the second segment is deleted. This corresponds to the fact that five left parentheses occur before the word *she*, but only four right parentheses. But if the cutting point is moved one word to the left, four constituents are damaged if either the first or the second segment is deleted. These constituents are: *on bail, being released on bail, after being released on bail,* and once again, the sentence itself. This corresponds to the fact that five left parentheses occur before the cutting point but only one right parenthesis. Thus, moving the cutting point one word to the left increased the number of damaged constituents from one to four. It is suggested that this indicates that the constraints placed on one segment by the other have correspondingly increased, and that the completion sets of either the LD or RD items associated with these cutting points have correspondingly decreased in size. This appears to be a reasonable result, as evidenced by the difference between items (8) and (9):

(8)   ..... she brooded over her arrest.
(9)   .... bail she brooded over her arrest.

If, instead of using a bracketing notation, the structure is presented in tree-form, as in Figure 1, it can be seen that the number of damaged constituents can be determined by counting the number of nodes which dominate terminal symbols in both segments of the sentence. These nodes will henceforth be referred to as T-nodes (since they traverse the cutting point). In Figure 1, four T-nodes are labelled as such, these T-

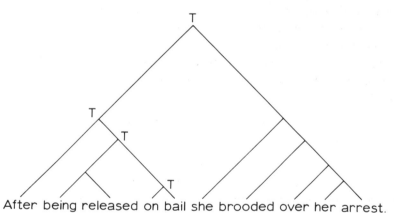

After being released on bail she brooded over her arrest.

Fig. 1.   T-nodes produced if cutting point for above sentence is located between
on and *bail.*

nodes being produced if the cutting point is located between *on* and *bail.* It will be seen that the number of T-nodes is necessarily the same whether we consider an LD or an RD item.

Obviously the number of T-nodes produced will only be an approximate index of the size of the completion set. The procedure takes no account of what type of node is involved, and it also ignores the operation of semantic variables. In addition, there will be many cases in which the subject is not required to reconstruct damaged constituents indicated by the presence of a T-node. As an extreme case, consider sentence (10), below. If this sentence is cut between *saw* and *the*, five T-nodes are produced:

(10)   ((All ((the people) (who (saw (the man))))) (left (the (party))))

But in item (11), which is the LD item derived from (10), the subject is quite at liberty to take *the man* as the subject of the verb *left*, rather than

(11)   ..... the man left the party.

as the object of some other verb, and at most needs to reconstruct only one constituent, instead of the postulated five.

If there are a relatively large number of cases such as this, the T-node count will not be a satisfactory index of completion set size. But in such cases the completions provided by the subjects can be examined to determine how many constituents were in fact reconstructed.

The T-node counts were determined in the following way. Eight structural descriptions of each sentence used to generate items were obtained. In some cases, these structural descriptions were limited to binary structures, and in some cases, they were not. The people assigning the structural descriptions ranged in sophistication from students with no knowledge of linguistics (but who were briefly instructed in the technique of assigning structures), to professional linguists. Thus for each sentence, there were eight separate estimates of the T-node count. Each of these estimates was then correlated with measures of the difficulty of the RD and LD items derived from these sentences.

All eight T-node estimates were significantly and positively correlated with the difficulty of LD items,[2] with a mean product-moment correlation coefficient of 0.50 and a range of 0.38 to 0.54. However, *none* of the eight T-node estimates were significantly correlated with the difficulty of RD items, the mean correlation being 0.06 with a range of 0.01 to 0.11. This discrepancy between the results for RD and LD items obviously raises some important issues. One possibility is that the T-node estimate derived from the original sentences was not a satisfactory index of the number of constituents reconstructed by subjects in the completion of RD items. But T-node estimates based on the structures of the sentences produced by the subjects themselves yielded exactly the same results.[3] A further possibility is that the estimates of item difficulty were in error. Since subjects worked with blocks of items, only indirect information about the difficulty of individual items was available. Accordingly, an additional experiment was carried out (Forster, 1966c) in which subjects were tested individually, and the time required to complete each item separately was recorded. But once again, exactly the same results were obtained: the T-node estimates predicted LD item difficulty quite well, but did not predict RD item difficulty. This experiment, however, provided an even more unexpected finding. When the agreement between the two experimental measures of the difficulty of each item was examined, it was found that the correlation for LD items was 0.64, but the correlation for RD items (0.06) did not differ significantly from zero. Faced with this result, the search for a correlate of RD item difficulty had to be abandoned.

Two assumptions are sufficient to account for the results just described: (1) assume that in the case of the RD item, a subject, once having read the item, is immediately capable of selecting one of a number of different ways of completing the item; (2) on the other hand, assume that in the case of the LD item, the subject must instead engage in some kind of trial and error search routine, selecting candidates for the completion, and then testing them for compatibility with the specified sequence of words. In the latter case, the fewer the number of potential completions, the longer the subject will take to locate one of them. Hence the correlation between the number of T-nodes and LD item difficulty is obtained. But in the case of RD items, since it is assumed that the subject already knows exactly how to complete the item (ignoring the problem of finding the correct number of words), then the size of the completion set should have no effect at all on item difficulty.[4] Thus the T-node count is uncorrelated with RD item difficulty. Furthermore, if the subject always knows how to complete any given RD item, then all RD items should be equivalent in difficulty, if factors such as the number of words to be written are equated. Hence any difference in the measured difficulty of two RD items can only reflect errors of measurement, and therefore, two experimentally independent measurements of the difficulty of the RD items will be uncorrelated.

Doubtless there are other possible interpretations, but this particular interpretation seems very plausible. The reader can judge this for himself by attempting the solutions of the following items. In items (12) and (13) below, the T-node count is low, whereas in (14) and (15), it is high. For the author, at least, the only item producing any hesitation in deciding on the general form of the completion is item (15)[5]:

(12)   Two weeks after the first good rain . . . .

(13)   . . . . in the camp a cry went up.

(14)   When she had completely exhausted all her own . . . .

(15)   . . . . . up as try any further.

Now the argument must be taken a step further, and the relevance of these interpretations to a theory of sentence production must be stated. The critical assumption involved is that the only information processing systems available to the subject for solution of the items are in fact those systems normally used in the tasks of sentence production or understanding. Doubtless it is quite possible that if subjects were given extended training in the solution of RD and LD items, new information processing systems could be developed (in which case we would expect the results of the experiments to change), but since the subjects received quite limited practice, the assumption is not unreasonable. It has already been proposed that the results are consistent with the view that sentence production takes place in the manner postulated by Yngve (1960). We shall return to this proposal later. A further suggestion links the results with sentence understanding rather than sentence production. Sentence understanding could equally well be viewed as a 'left to right' process. That is, the hearer should be quite accustomed to analyzing sentences on the basis of cues provided by the beginning of the sentence (and in the absence of cues provided by the end), but should be relatively unaccustomed to analyzing sentences on the basis of cues provided by the end of the sentence alone. Thus, in the case of RD items, the subject anticipates the possible ways in which the sentence could proceed. But in the case of LD items, no such anticipation is involved. More specifically, this interpretation requires that the subjects can more readily identify the nature of a constituent if the beginning of the constituent is known, than if only the end of the constituent is known. A third possibility is that item difficulty is solely a function of the nature of the constituents presented to the subject. For example, the RD–LD difference may be explained on the assumption that RD items in English will usually contain the subject, and often the verb, whereas LD items will do so only rarely. This particular interpretation does not adequately cover the facts. First, it is doubtful whether the content of any item is systematically associated with any particular type of constituent. Second, the theory cannot explain the statistical independence of two measurements of RD item difficulty. Furthermore, when each item is classified according to whether the item contains a subject of a clause, or a verb, both of these, or none of these, it can be shown this classification system is unrelated to either RD or LD item difficulty. As far as English is concerned, this interpretation of the results seems to be unlikely.

Before any further attempt is made to decide on a satisfactory interpretation, we should consider further available evidence which bears on the issues involved. Of considerable importance is the question of the generality of the results. Is the RD–LD difference merely a characteristic of English, or is it found in all languages? Rather than simply selecting languages at random, it was decided to select a language which exhibited structures that would be found only rarely in English. An obvious example would be one of the so-called left-branching languages, such as Turkish.[6] Accordingly, it was decided to repeat the experiment, using Turkish sentences and Turkish native-speakers as subjects (Forster, 1966a).

Every attempt was made to ensure that the conditions of the Turkish experiment were the same as those for the English experiment. The subjects were college students, the sentences were drawn from comparable sources, and were arranged in blocks of items as before. The responses were scored in the same way by a Turkish native-speaker. However, in this experiment, out of the total of 62 subjects taking part in the experiment, 15 obtained a higher score for LD items than for RD items. The mean score per block of RD items was 4.11 as opposed to a mean score of 3.53 for LD items. The statistical analysis of these results showed that, once again, LD items were significantly more difficult to complete than RD items, but that the Turkish results differed from the English results in that the magnitude of the RD–LD difference was significantly smaller for Turkish. Such a reduction in the RD–LD difference was also observed in English when the length constraint was removed. In this case, it was assumed that this reduction was due to a reduction in item difficulty. Such an argument cannot be applied to the Turkish results, since in general, the Turkish subjects obtained lower scores than did the English-speaking subjects. Furthermore, the Turkish subjects obtained higher scores for LD items than did the English-speaking subjects, but obtained lower scores for the RD items.

These results suggest that both left and right-branching languages demonstrate the RD–LD difference, but that in left-branching languages this difference is reduced in size. How does such a result bear upon the theoretical argument? First, it eliminates any argument predicated on the simple assumption that the RD–LD difference is due solely to the fact that sentences involve a linear time sequence. Obviously, sentences in Turkish proceed in a linear sequence with respect to time in exactly the same way as they do in English. Similarly, the results eliminate any argument based on the assumption that speakers utilize a system which specifies transitional probabilities between elements of the sentence, whether these elements be taken as words or word-types (the results from Turkish or English alone would have been consistent which such a view), since this argument is unable to account for the marked reduction in the Turkish RD–LD difference. These results also appear to eliminate the argument based on the assumption that subjects could more readily identify constituents when the beginning was known than when only the end of the constituent was known. Consider a sentence which produces N incomplete constituents when the first or second half is deleted. In the LD item derived from such a sentence, there will be N constituents of which the beginning is not known, whether the original sentence was left or right-branching in structure. Hence this interpretation also requires an equal effect for both languages.

One theoretical avenue is not eliminated by these results. Consider the problem of designing a machine which would be capable of solving LD and RD items. The simplest, but least efficient method would be to design an algorithm which enumerated the sentences of the language, producing as output the first sentence encountered which matched the constraints imposed by the item. A considerable improvement in efficiency would be obtained if this system were allowed to determine whether the sentence currently being synthesized would be likely to meet the constraints, rejecting it immediately if this probability fell below some prescribed value. If we use as a component of this system the device described by Yngve (1960, 1961), some interesting results are obtained. This device processes the information provided by a context-free phrase-structure grammar in such a way that, as far as possible, the order in which terminal symbols appear in the synthesis of the sentence matches the order in which they are to appear in the sentence itself. If we think of this device as progressing through the tree representing the surface structure of the sentence, it will always begin at the topmost node of the tree, and on each occasion that a branch is encountered, it descends first via the left-hand path. Each time it does so, it places in temporary storage the information required to ensure that when the device eventually retraces its steps (having reached a terminal symbol) it will descend via the right-hand path of that branch.

Assume that this device is attempting to solve RD items in a language where all formation rules are either of the form $A \rightarrow bC$ or $A \rightarrow b$ (i.e., a totally right-branching language). The first operation in the synthesis of a sentence will specify the first terminal symbol of the sentence. This symbol could be immediately compared with the first word of the item, and if these do not match, this attempted solution could be rejected, and a different initial operation selected. Once the sequence of operations necessary to satisfy the constraints imposed has been discovered, the device is free (except for the length constraint) to proceed in any way consistent with the grammar. Thus, once this stage has been reached, the time required to produce a completion would be the same, whether there was only one way in which the machine could proceed, or many. However, if the device were attempting to solve LD items in such a language, many more operations would be required before it could be determined whether the attempted solution was feasible. If the LD item consisted of six blanks followed by six words, the device would have to continue the task of specifying in order the words of each attempted solution until the seventh word was reached. Only then would it be able to decide whether the attempted solution should be rejected or continued. Moreover, the greater the number of different ways in which an acceptable completion could be synthesized, the more rapidly the device should lacate an acceptable completion. Thus, in such a language, LD items would clearly be more difficult to complete than RD items. Moreover, the size of the completion set would not affect solution time for RD items, but would affect solution time for LD items.[7]

These results are exactly reversed if the language is such that all formation rules are of the form $A \rightarrow Cb$ or $A \rightarrow b$ (i.e., a totally left-branching language). In this case, the first operation in the synthesis of a sentence will specify the last word of the sentence, and hence it will be the LD item which permits rapid evaluation of the adequacy of a given attempt at solution. Thus, for the left-branching language, LD items will be easier to complete than RD items, and completion set size will affect solution times for RD items, but not LD items.

Obviously, this is an extremely simple model, and is not proposed as a serious theory of the information processing systems actually used by subjects. However, it does serve as a starting point, and deficiencies in the model can be corrected when it becomes apparent that the model is inconsistent with known facts. First and foremost among these facts is that no natural language conforms to the requirements of the two languages described. But it may be possible to generalize the argument to cover the properties actually possessed by natural languages in the following way. The critical feature of the argument is the postulated relationship between the order in which terminal symbols are produced and the relative difficulty of RD and LD items. This relationship is as follows: if the terminal symbols specified by the particular item under consideration tend normally to be produced relatively early in the synthesis of a sentence, then the time required to reach solution is reduced. This can be stated in another way: if the order in which terminal symbols are produced in the synthesis of a sentence closely approximates the order in which they appear in the actual sentence, then RD items based on such a sentence will be easier to complete than LD items. Any discrepancy between these two orders can be assumed to reduce the difference between RD and LD items.

A simple index of the relationship between the order of appearance of terminal symbols in the left to right synthesis and the order of appearance in the finished version of the sentence is provided by the rank-order correlation coefficient. If there is a perfect match (as in the case the totally right-branching language), the correlation is 1.0. If one order is exactly the reverse of another (as in the case of the totally left-branching language), the correlation is −1.0. This index will be referred to as the LR index. In order to calculate the value of the LR index for any particular sentence, one takes the three associated with the surface structure of the sentence, and traces through the tree in the manner described by Yngve (1961), noting the order in which terminal symbols are produced.[8] This order is then correlated with the order in which these symbols are realized as words in the sentence. Theoretically, a left-branching language would produce negative LR indices but, as Miller and Chomsky (1963) have observed, such languages exhibit both left- and right-branching structures. However, any tendency for left-branching to occur will tend to lower the value of the LR indices obtained. Thus the hypothesis resulting from the model is as follows: there will be a positive correlation between the RD-LD difference obtained for a language and the mean value of the LR indices of a sample of sentences in that language.

Since this hypothesis can scarcely be assessed on the basis of only two languages, it was decided to collect data for two additional languages (Forster, 1966d). Japanese was selected as a further example of a left-branching language, and German was chosen as a further example of a right-branching language. It was hoped that German would occupy a position between English and Turkish with respect to the mean LR index, and thus provide the possibility of mapping in more detail the relationship between the RD-LD differences and the LR indices.

As before, every effort was made to ensure that the conditions of these experiments would be comparable to those of the Turkish and English experiments. The only serious departure in the details of the procedure occurred in the case of the Japanese experiment. Since the concept of a word is not easily defined in Japanese, it proved difficult to specify the length of the completion. This was attempted in terms of the concept of a 'dictionary form', but since two Japanese speakers will not always agree as to the number of such forms in a sentence, the responses were regarded as adequate if they approximated the specified length. The LR indices were determined on the basis of structures assigned to each sentence in each language by two speakers of the language. The knowledge of linguistics of these speakers varied considerably, and hence the adequacy of the structures assigned may also have varied considerably. However, their only relevant properties for our purposes are the value of the LR index and the value of the T-node count.

After averaging the obtained LR indices over the forty sentences of each language used in the experiment,[9] the following mean values were obtained: English, 0.95; German, 0.83; Japanese, 0.75; Turkish, 0.62. According to the hypothesis, we should find that German shows a smaller RD-LD difference than English, followed by Japanese and then Turkish. This expectation was confirmed. For German, the mean score per block of items was 4.18, and for LD items it was 2.73. RD items yielded a mean score of 4.91 for Japanese, and LD items yielded a mean of 3.73 (as in previous analyses, LD items were significantly more difficult to complete than RD items for both German and Japanese). Thus, the RD-LD differences for English, German, Japanese and Turkish were 2.22, 1.45, 1.18 and 0.58 respectively.[10]

Closer analysis of these data provided an unexpected result. Table I

TABLE I

Mean score per item for samples of high and low T-node items

	High T-node items			Low T-node items		
	RD	LD	RD–LD	RD	LD	RD–LD
English	1.12	0.36	0.76	1.18	0.83	0.35
German	0.72	0.41	0.31	0.99	0.59	0.40
Japanese	0.93	0.76	0.17	1.03	0.82	0.21
Turkish	0.61	0.57	0.04	1.00	0.68	0.32

shows the mean score per item (total possible score now being 2) for comparable samples of items having either a relatively high mean T-node count or a relatively low mean T-node count. For low T-node items, the small differences between the results for the four languages are not statistically reliable. But for high T-node items, the differences are substantial, and also are statistically significant. In general, all four languages show the tendency for high T-node items to be more diffcult than low T-node items, but it can be seen that for English, an increase in the T-node count leads to an increase in the RD–LD difference, whereas for the other three languages, it leads to a decrease in the RD–LD difference.

It is clear that the RD–LD difference is a positive function of the LR index only in the case of high T-node items. It may be that the constancy of the low T-node item results reflects the fact that since there are assumed to be a relatively large number of ways in which such items could be completed, no special advantage accrues to either LD or RD items by virtue of the branching characteristics of the language. Of course, this argument fails to explain why the low T-node item RD–LD differences are all positive.

It will be recalled that a further result of the application of an Yngve sentence producer to the task of solving items was that, for totally right-branching languages, the difficulty of RD items would not be affected by the size of the completion set, whereas the difficulty of LD items would be affected. It has already been noted that this effect occurs in English. However, for totally left-branching languages, precisely the reverse result should be obtained. This observation suggests the possibility that as the LR index of a language decreases, we should find that the effect of the number of T-nodes on LD item difficulty increases relative to the effect of the number of T-nodes on RD item difficulty. Examination of the results shows precisely this trend. For English, the effect of the number of T-nodes on RD item difficulty is less than half as great as the effect on LD item difficulty. This situation changes as a function of the LR index, and in the extreme case, for Turkish, the effect of the number of T-nodes on RD items is substantially greater than the effect on LD items.

Much of what has been said so far depends on the assumption that the 'left to right' sentence generator proposed by Yngve provides a plausible model of sentence production. This view can be challenged in a number of ways. First and foremost, the model does not mention any relationship between decisions made by the speaker concerning the content of the message and the actual process of constructing the sentence. Second, as Miller and Chomsky (1963) have pointed out, there is no reason to assume that speakers must always select major phrase-types before selecting lower level constituents. Furthermore, this strict top-to-bottom method of construction implies that left-branching sentences should be especially difficult to produce, since each left-branch increases the load on temporary storage by one symbol. However, the existence of markedly left-branching constructions in languages such as Turkish and Japanese, which do not appear in any way to be difficult for speakers of these languages, argues against the validity of such a conclusion.[11]

Third, this particular type of sentence producer is based upon a context-free phrase structure grammar, and it has been shown that such a grammar is inadequate for the task of describing the speaker's knowledge of his language (e.g., see Chomsky, 1961; Postal, 1964).

Following Katz and Postal (1964), it might be suggested that the sentence producer be provided with an input which is equivalent to the output of a sentence recognition device – namely, a semantic interpretation of the sentence. One could then view sentence production as a procedure for selecting a deep structure with the intended interpretation, followed by a relatively straightforward conversion of this deep structure into a surface structure. However, such a view clearly implies that the speaker knows a great deal about the syntactic structure of the sentence to be produced prior to the output of any of the words of the sentence, and it is difficult to see how such a system could account for the results described in this paper. An alternative (and admittedly vague) proposal is to imagine the device being equipped with a set of functions which effectively enable the speaker to short-circuit this sequence of computational steps, and to directly infer the surface characteristics of the sentence in a 'left to right' manner. Thus, if the input to the device is such that a yes-no question is called for, the speaker can immediately determine that the first formative in the sentence will be an auxiliary verb, and furthermore the speaker will be able to determine correctly the tense and number of this auxiliary without having considered in detail the structure of the remainder of the sentence. Or, if a passive is called for, the speaker can immediately focus on the precise format of what would be the object noun-phrase in the deep structure, since he knows this will appear first in the sentence.

If such a view proves to be reasonable, and it is not too difficult to sketch the outlines of the necessary short-circuiting functions, then the following suggestion can be made. If we take the surface structure of any sentence and assign numbers to the nodes of this structure according to the order in which these nodes would be determined by an Yngve generator, then the resulting tree will provide a partial description of the sequence of operations performed in the construction of the sentence by a device equipped with the appropriate input and short-circuiting functions.[12] The description will be incomplete in the sense that it omits the computational steps performed by the short-circuiting functions which will intervene between the steps that are mentioned in the description.

However, it may be objected that postulating these special functions already undermines the basic assumption of an Yngve generator, namely, that the surface tree is constructed strictly from top-to-bottom. Such functions would certainly be powerful enough to remove the necessity for traversing left-recursive structures in this way, and it is not difficult to show that the appropriate functions exist. For example, Chomsky's optimal perceptual device (Chomsky, 1963) has the capacity to move in either direction through the tree, and viewed as a component of a production system, it can compute left-branching structures as easily as right-branching structures. If it is conceded that the device ought to include such a feature, then clearly there is no basis for the claim that the modified Yngve generator can account for the results of the sentence completion experiments. In the case of the hypothetical language where all formation rules were of the form $A \to Cb$ or $A \to b$, the first operation of the device would not determine the last word of the sentence at all, but would presumably (if the device were optimally designed) determine the first word of the sentence. Hence there is no reason to expect the sentence completion results for left-branching languages to differ from the results for right-branching languages.

In considering arguments of this kind, it quickly becomes apparent that it is very difficult to draw conclusions for any cases except the extremes. What if only some of the constructions found in surface trees are left-branching? What if the device is not optimally designed? In order to explore these questions in more detail, one must develop a far more rigorous theory of the relationship between surface structure and the information processing assumed to be involved in the sentence completion experiment. However, this has not proved to be a simple task. As a consequence, we have resorted to the strategy of building machines with the desired properties and investigating their behavior when faced with the same task as the human subjects.

As a first approximation, it has been assumed that nothing of vital importance will be overlooked if we ignore the problem of specifying the input to the sentence producer, or if we omit the details of the special functions that enable the device to directly infer surface structure. Thus, in effect, we construct a machine based on a context-free phrase structure grammar – i.e., a push-down store automaton (Chomsky, 1963;

Evey, 1963). The grammars on which these automata are based are constructed in the following way. For any nonterminal symbol in the grammar, consider the longest string of terminal symbols that can be derived from this symbol without any recursive steps in the derivation. If, for any rule of the grammar $A \rightarrow BC$, it is the case that C tends to permit the derivation of a longer string than does B, then the grammar will be said to be right-branching. Once a grammar meeting this requirement has been constructed, a left-branching grammar can be constructed by substituting for each rule of the form $A \rightarrow BC$ a rule of the form $A \rightarrow CB$. In all respects except their branching characteristics, the two grammars formed in this way will be perfectly equivalent. Next, using the algorithm described by Evey (1963), two left-to-right push-down store transducers are constructed for each grammar: one which accepts a terminal string as input and produces as output a list of the rules used in the construction of the string, and one which accepts this rule-list as input and produces from left to right the terminal string associated with this input.

The sentence completion experiment is then carried out by presenting these automata with RD or LD sentence fragments. The analysis routine attempts to make the most economical analysis of the fragment, and the production routine uses this information to synthesize a sentence meeting the constraints imposed, resorting to a random search procedure in the absence of any relevant information.

Although these experiments have not been completed, a general pattern appears to be emerging. As would be expected, these automata (when represented as computer programs) take longer to complete LD items. When the number of T-nodes is kept to a minimum, the RD–LD differences are constant for a variety of automata based on right-branching grammars. However, when the T-node count increases, the RD–LD difference for automata based on left-branching grammars decreases relative to the effect found for automata based on right-branching grammars. For the right-branching case, it appears that the T-node count is irrelevant to the time required to solve RD tems, but is positively correlated with the difficulty of LD items. These findings are consistent with the pattern established for English on human subjects. However, for the left-branching case, no clear patterns have emerged.

So far, it appears that these results are also found for automata in which the strict top-to-bottom constraint is relaxed for left-recursive structures. For example, if the grammar contains the following expansion rules for the symbol A: (1) $A \rightarrow Aa$, (2) $A \rightarrow Ab$, (3) $A \rightarrow BC$, then the strict top-to-bottom constraint would require that the structure:

$$((((BC)a)b)a)$$

be developed by applying the rules in the sequence: 1, 2, 1 and 3. But if this constraint is relaxed, it is possible to design the automaton so that exactly the reverse sequence is used, and the structure is developed from bottom-to-top. Although this procedure eliminates the burden on memory capacity imposed by left-recursive structures, it will not work for non-recursive left-branching cases, such as the following sequence of rules: (1) $A \rightarrow Ba$, (2) $B \rightarrow Cb$, (3) $C \rightarrow Dc$, (4) $D \rightarrow Ed$, etc. In these cases, more complex strategies are required. One method of coping with these problems would be to base the automaton on the so-called standard form of the grammar (Greibach, 1965), where all formation rules become right-branching. However, it appears that under these conditions it is impossible to distinguish between the sentence completion performance of automata based on right-branching grammars and automata based on the standard form of left-branching grammars. In passing, it may be noted that, to date, the most interesting failure of the model being proposed involves a further type of item, where every alternate word is deleted, as in (16):

(16)   – no – to – us, – dropped – down – our – on – ground.

The machine time required to reach solution for items of this type agrees quite well with reported intuitions: these items fall between RD and LD items in difficulty. However, for human subjects, these items prove to be far more difficult than LD items (Forster, 1964).

Although exploratory research of this kind is obviously relevant, it must be remembered that it begs the question of whether the sentence completion experiment reveals any significant properties of the sentence production device. Given the uncertainty in the field, the mere demonstration that one particular configuration of analysis and synthesis automata is capable of accounting for some of the data is not particularly impressive. We have mentioned earlier that the results of the experiments may in fact be more relevant to a theory of sentence understanding. One version of this theory asserts that the sentence fragments represented by RD and LD items are not equally informative concerning the meaning of the total sentence from which the fragments were formed. Presumably, such a view can be tested by providing the subjects with this information in the form of a paraphrase of the total sentence. Under these conditions, we should find that LD items are now no more difficult to complete than RD items. For example, different groups of subjects could be given either item (18) or item (19) but, before attempting the completion, they are also given the paraphrase contained in (17), and are instructed to complete the item so that the sentence produced has roughly the same meaning as the paraphrase.

(17)   A large crowd chased him; they went past the gates of the city, and then went on for three miles.

(18)   He was chased for three miles beyond . . . .

(19)   . . . . the city gates by a large crowd.

The results of a preliminary experiment provide little support for the view in question. For a group of naval recruits, the paraphrase condition produced mean solution times of 60.1 s and 83.0 s for RD and LD items respectively. Baseline measures of the time required for the same subjects to solve comparable items with no paraphrase yielded means of 49.1 s for RD items and 76.3 s for LD items (all items used in this experiment had high T-node counts). Thus the major effect of the paraphrase is to increase the time required to find a solution.

A more interesting variant of the proposal, that an explanation of the difficulty of LD items should be phrased in terms of sentence recognition processes, has been suggested by J. A. Fodor. In this case, it is argued that the sentence fragments represented by RD and LD items are not equally informative with respect to the lexically marked cues to the deep structure of the sentence. Fodor and Garrett (1967) have argued that sentence recognition should be viewed as a process by which the hearer employs heuristics to directly infer the deep structure of a sentence from surface structure cues. It is argued that the lexical entries associated with formatives will contain information concerning the possible deep structure configurations that such formatives can enter into. Further, for any construction, it will usually be the head of that construction which is marked in the lexicon for the types of deep structure trees with which it can be associated. Thus, if we consider verb-complement constructions, it will be the verb that is marked in the lexicon with respect to the complements it can take, and there will be no way of marking the complements with respect to the verbs that can be associated with them. For example, consider items (20) and (21), derived from the one sentence:

(20)   All the children were watching . . . . .
(21)   . . . . . the man sweep the floor.

Item (20) causes little problem, since the verb is present and all the necessary information is available. But in (21) the verb is missing, and although the fragment may be correctly analyzed as a sentence embedded in a verb phrase, there is no direct method for inferring the nature of the preceding verb. Note that it would be easy to design a device that *was* able to do this: a simple list of complement types and the verbs associated with them would be sufficient. But the point of Fodor and Garrett's remarks is that speakers of a language are hypothesized not to possess such heuristics. The importance of such an argument becomes clear when it is considered that the left-branching languages differ from right-branching languages in just the relevant respect: they tend to be verb-final. Thus, the complement would precede the verb in Turkish and Japanese, and hence the situation observed in items (20) and (21) would be exactly reversed. In left-branching languages, it would be more likely that the LD item would contain the verb.

Thus the subject's task in the sentence completion experiment is to recover as much of the deep structure of the total sentence as possible, filling in the gaps in any order, as necessary. Obviously, where more of the structure can be directly inferred, the task of completion is relatively simple. For right-branching languages, LD items will be more difficult because important lexical cues to the deep structure have been deleted. But in left-branching languages, this effect will be lessened somewhat, since the LD item will still contain many of the important cues. Of course, the argument will have to be extended to cover cases other than the verb. As far as we can determine, the difficulty of the following items has very little to do with the fact that the nature of the matrix verb is unknown.

(22)   . . . . themselves, live on other fish which do.
(23)   . . . . basic to this book and writing it.

(24)   .... committee as we had pushed Alan's through.
(25)   .... any cattle, but with nine large boxes.

Given that such an extension is possible, it should be observed that the force of the argument is that the sentence completion results can be accounted for without making any assumptions about sentence production.

In some respects, it is hard to determine whether this interpretation of the results can be clearly distinguished from the account offered in terms of a sentence production device. This difficulty stems from the fact that it is easy to show that a sentence production theory must also include an account of the information provided by the analysis of the sentence fragment. For example, consider the sequence of operations involved in the 'left to right' planning of a sentence. Let this sequence be represented as $\phi_1, \phi_2, ..., \phi_i, ..., \phi_n$. Whether a particular item is difficult to complete or not depends on which subset of these operations the subject of the experiment can identify from an analysis of the sentence fragment. If he identifies the sequence $\phi_j, \phi_{j+1}, ..., \phi_i, \phi_{i+1}, ..., \phi_{m-1}, \phi_m$ where $m \leqslant n$, then the item is easiest to complete when $j = 1$, and the difficulty of the item increases as a function of j. Also, even under the condition where $j = 1$, if there is any ϕ_i such that the next operation defined is ϕ_k where $k > i + 1$, then the difficulty of the item increases as a function of the expression $k - i$.[13] Thus it can be argued that the point of the demonstration concerning verbs and complements mentioned above is that, in both right- and left-branching languages, the verb is planned before the complement. Hence information concerning the verb will be more useful since it identifies an earlier operation in the synthesis of the sentence. The reason for assuming that in left-branching languages the verb is planned before the complement, even though their order of appearance in the sentence is reversed, is just precisely the fact that the surface structure in these cases is left-branching.

It may be suspected that this discussion exposes a very basic weakness – namely, that it may not be possible to discuss intelligibly whether a particular set of experimental results is a function of one type of system or another. That is, the connection between sentence recognition and sentence production may be so intimate that they can at best be regarded as different aspects of the same system. However, there may be some facts which are relevant. For example, when the lexical content of RD and LD items is identical, there is still a small difference in the difficulty of the items (Forster, 1966a). Again, in an unpublished study, it has been shown that if the subject is provided with a list of the words to be used in the completion (the order of the words being scrambled), there is still a small difference in the predicted direction for items where the T-node count is high. Presumably under these circumstances, the subject is not deprived of lexical cues to the deep structure, although of course, any cues provided by the ordering of the lexical items will be eliminated. A further problem is encountered when it is asked how the subject manages to find a completion when the appropriate cues to deep structure are missing. Here we have the choice of saying either that the subject searches through the set of possible analyses of the total sentence, or that the subject searches through the set of possible ways of constructing the sentence. It seems very doubtful that it would be sensible to regard these alternatives as radically different. Generally speaking, however, the crucial issue involves the interpretation assigned to the output of the analysis routine. The sentence production view claims that this output will be useful to the degree that it establishes the earliest operations involved in the left to right planning of the sentence. The alternative view claims that this output is useful to the degree that the informs the subject of the detail of the deep structure of the total sentence. Much of the difficulty in separating these views stems from the fact that the features of the analysis output that are informative according to one view would also be informative according to the other.

In conclusion, it must be acknowledged that the data presented in this paper do not unequivocally support any one particular view of language processing, and this is hardly surprising. It would be claimed, however, that the data are suggestive in the sense that they would be compatible with only a relatively small range of theories. If it transpires that the explanation of these results becomes deeply and inextricably embedded in a general theory of problem-solving, with less and less reference being made to linguistic abilities, then the significance of these studies will thereby be diminished.

Department of Psychology,
Monash University,
Clayton, Victoria, Australia.

NOTES

* This paper was prepared while the author was a Research Fellow at the University of Melbourne, Victoria, Australia. The research' reported was made possible by the generous technical assistance of the following people, to whom the author wishes to express his gratitude: R. B. Lees, Belan Togrol, D. Cuceloglu, Toshio Iritani, Miho Steinberg, P. Tanaka, J. Oki, E. E. Davis, N. Viernstein, M. Clyne and M. Garrett.

[1] An obvious suggestion is to present the subject of an experiment with some stimulus display, and ask him to comment on it. In this way, the semantic content, and perhaps even the sentence-type of the observed utterance may be controlled (e.g., Turner and Rommetveit, 1967). But this would not reveal how the speaker actually synthesized the sentence, once he had decided what to say, and which sentence-type to use.

[2] An incidental result of interest was that there was no evidence that any one method of assigning structures was more highly correlated with LD item difficulty than any other. For example, binary structures were equivalent to structures with multiple branching. Also, the results obtained from linguists were equivalent to the results obtained from non-linguists.

[3] It should be noted that these T-node estimates were not more highly correlated with LD item difficulty than the T-node estimates based on the original sentences.

[4] This will hold only for what might be called 'normal' sentences. No doubt an RD item such as *What what what he wanted cost...* will be more difficult to complete than any of the RD items used in these experiments.

[5] It should be stressed that we are not attempting to provide an exhaustive account of why some items are difficult and why some are not. Undoubtedly there are many variables, apart from the T-node count, which control the difficulty of LD items, but these will not be discussed here.

[6] The suggestion for such an experiment was first made by R. B. Lees.

[7] It is important to note that these results would not be obtained if the restrictions on the operation of the device were relaxed. For example, if the device were free to expand any nonterminal symbol, rather than only the left-most, then LD items would be no more difficult than RD items, and the T-node count would be of no relevance to the difficulty of either type of item.

[8] Here thought of as word-types rather than words or morphemes. The sentence planning operation is said to produce a terminal symbol when the rule producing that symbol is first selected.

[9] The mean LR indices for the two speakers assigning structures in each language showed reasonable agreement in all cases except for Turkish, where a wide discrepancy was found. The reason for this is not clear, but may indicate that the LR index is sensitive to the type of structure assigned. In spite of this discrepancy, the mean LR index for each language was determined by averaging the values provided by the two speakers assigning structures.

[10] It does not seem possible to account for these results on the assumption that the more difficult a set of items is, the greater will be the RD–LD difference. The subjects in the English experiment obtained the highest overall score, but also obtained the largest RD–LD difference. The German subjects produced the next largest RD–LD difference, but obtained the lowest overall score. It is also difficult to attribute the results to differences in the people scoring the responses. When *all* responses were scored by a single person who considered only whether the item was completed (ignoring whether the completion was grammatical), precisely the same relationships between the language were obtained.

[11] However, an argument can be made that very few sentences involve a load on memory greater than the limit suggested by Yngve (1961), and that the sentences which do exceed

this limit are most unlikely to be used in free speech. But even if this observation is correct, it would still be expected that a sentence involving a memory load, of, say, six symbols should be more difficult to say than a sentence involving a memory load of only one symbol. Purely informal evidence suggests that this is not the case. Of course, it may be easy to show that this is true of English. For example, the sentence *John's uncle's book's cover's front's color is red* has a depth of six, and would be harder to say than a sentence with lesser depth. But this may simply indicate that English speakers are totally unaccustomed to developing structures of this kind beyond a depth of two or three.

[12] Whereas the Yngve generator can be expressed as a push-down store automaton, it is doubtless the case that the device being proposed here would have to be more powerful, and thus could not be so expressed.

[13] As indicated by the fact that if the center of the sentence is deleted, leaving just the first and last quarters of the sentence, the difficulty of completion is approximately equal to that of LD items (Forster, 1964).

BIBLIOGRAPHY

Chomsky, N., 'On the Notion 'Rule of Grammar'', in R. Jakobsen (ed.), *Structure of Language and its Mathematical Axpects, Proc. 12th Symp. in App. Math.*, American Mathematical Society, Providence, R.I., 1961.

Chomsky, N., 'Formal Properties of Grammars', in R. D. Luce, R. R. Bush and E. Galanter (eds.), *Handbook of Mathematical Psychology*, Vol. II, Wiley, New York, 1963.

Evey, J., *The Theory and Application of Pushdown Store Machines*, Rep. No. NSF-10, Harvard Compl. Lab., Cambridge, 1963.

Fodor, J. A. and Garrett, M., 'Some Syntactic Determinants of Sentential Complexity', *Perception and Psychophysics* 2 (1967) 289–296.

Forster, K. I., *Left-to-Right Processes in the Construction of Sentences*, unpublished doctoral dissertation, University of Illinois, 1964.

Forster, K. I., 'Left-to-Right Processes in the Construction of Sentences', *J. verb. Learn. verb. Behav.* 5 (1966) 285–291. (a)

Forster, K. I., 'The Effect of Removal of Length Constraint on Sentence Completion Times', *J. verb. Learn. verb. Behav.* (in press), 1966 (b).

Forster, K. I., 'Sentence Completion Latencies as a Function of Constituent Structure', *J. verb. Learn. verb. Behav.* (in press), 1966 (c).

Forster, K. I., 'Sentence Completion in Left- and Right-Branching Languages', *J. verb. Learn. verb. Behav.* (in press), 1966 (d).

Greibach, S., 'A New Normal-Form Theorem for Context-free Phrase Structure Grammar', *J. Assoc. Comp. Mach.* 12 (1965) 42–52.

Guilford, J. P., 'Three Faces of Intellect', *Amer. Psychologist* 14 (1959) 469–479.

Johnson, N. F., 'Linguistic Models and Functional Units of Language Behavior', in S. Rosenberg (ed.), *Directions in Psycholinguistics*, Macmillan, New York, 1965.

Katz, J. J. and Postal, P. M., *An Integrated Theory of Linguistic Descriptions*, MIT Press, Cambridge, Mass., 1964.

Maclay, H. and Osgood, C. E., 'Hesitation Phenomena in Spontaneous English Speech', *Word* 15 (1959) 19–44.

Mehler, J., 'Some Effects of Grammatical Transformations on the Recall of English Sentences', *J. verb. Learn. verb. Behav.* 2 (1963) 346–351.

Miller, G. A. and Chomsky, N., 'Finitary Models of Language Users', in R. D. Luce, R. R.

Bush and E. Galanter (eds.), *Handbook of Mathematical Psychology*, Vol. II, Wiley, New York, 1963.

Postal, P., 'Limitations of Phrase Structure Grammars', in J. A. Fodor and J. J. Katz (eds.), *The Structure of Language*, Prentice-Hall, Englewood Cliffs, N.J., 1964.

Turner, E. A. and Rommetveit, R., 'Experimental Manipulation of the Production of Active and Passive Voice in Children', *Language and Speech* **10** (1967) 169–180.

Yngve, V. H., 'A Model and an Hypothesis for Language Structure', *Proc. Am. Phil. Soc.* **104** (1960) 444–466.

Yngve, V. H., 'The Depth Hypothesis', in R. Jakobsen (ed.), *Structure of Language and Its Mathematical Aspects, Proc. 12th Symp. in App. Math.*, American Mathematical Society, Providence, R.I., 1961.

INFORMATION, DECISION, AND THE SCIENTIST*

ABSTRACT. Decision-theoretical critique of 'semantic information' measures and of some other suggestions made by students of inductive logic leads to a formal statement of the following sequence of the scientist's choices:

(1) 'What Problem shall I study?' – chosing one of the sets of states of Nature 'payoff-relevant' to the scientist.

(2) 'What set of mutually exclusive and exhaustive Hypotheses shall I test?' – chosing a partition of the Problem set.

(3) 'What kind of Evidence shall I use?' – chosing a set of observations presumably related statistically to the set of Hypotheses.

(4) 'What Rule for accepting a hypothesis shall I use?'. (For a certain class of the scientist's payoff functions, the Rule is to accept a hypothesis with maximal posterior probability.)

To be optimal the four choices must be made simultaneously and will depend on the payoff functions for the alternative Problems, on the initial probabilities of states of Nature, and on the costs of testing, computing, storing and communicating (the latter costs are related to 'teachability' or 'simplicity').

INTRODUCTION

The present author, an economist and statistician, has been mostly concerned with the choice of actions (policies, decisions). The result of an action depends not only on itself but also on the state of the outside world, seldom known with all the detail and precision needed to choose the best action. If actions include the getting of evidence about the outside world, the result of a chosen action – or rather of a chosen sequence of actions, including the gathering of evidence – may presumably be improved, even if the evidence still does not provide all the needed detail or is not completely reliable.

A scientist, too, is a choice-maker. He is said to choose between hypotheses. And he does use evidence. Philosophers of science have discussed criteria for the choice between hypotheses. As far as I can see they have asked two different questions;

(A)   What hypothesis should be tested?
(B)   What hypothesis should be accepted?

Note that the actions between which the choice must be made are quite different in (A) and in (B). Yet considerable perplexity was created in the literature, it would seem, (and as was pointed out in the more recent work of Carnap [8], and Bar-Hillel [5]) because it was thought necessary or useful to rank-order all hypotheses of a given set by combining the choice criteria for A and for B into one. Moreover I shall later show that it is useful, while maintaining Question B, to replace A by the following two questions:

(A1)   What set of mutually exclusive and exhaustive hypotheses should be tested?

(A2)   What kind of evidence should be collected for the test?

One criterion for Question (A), proposed in the literature was the comparative strength of two hypotheses: if hypothesis h_1 is strictly stronger than (i.e., if it strictly implies) hypothesis h_2, choose h_1 as the one to be tested. It seems indeed appropriate to say that h_1 'provides more information' than does h_2: for if you know that h_1 is true you also know that h_2 is true, while the converse is not true. Popper [40] pioneered with the example of $h_1 =$ 'the orbit is a circle', $h_2 =$ 'the orbit is an ellipse' (and thus possibly a circle). It is also notable that, a priori, (i.e., before the test) the stronger hypothesis is less probable than the weaker one since, denoting by $h_2 - h_1$ the (not impossible) hypothesis that the orbit is an ellipse with unequal axes, we have, in an obvious notation,

$$p(h_2) = p(h_1) + p(h_2 - h_1).^1$$

However the criterion of comparative strength, in the sense of the implication relation, induces only partial ordering on a given set of hypotheses. For it cannot apply to every pair of such hypotheses. For example, of the two above hypotheses, h_1 and $h_2 - h_1$, neither implies the other. To induce complete ordering, a less restrictive criterion was proposed: of two hypotheses choose one that implies a larger number of hypotheses (and is, in this sense, 'more falsifiable'). A still less restrictive and also completely ordering criterion (which, under certain assumptions, can be derived from the previous one) is this: choose the hypothesis which is, a priori, less probable (and in this sense 'more surprising'). In essence, this proposal was so derived also by Bar-Hillel and Carnap in their early work [3], much revised since. "And nothing pleaseth but rare accidents," said Shakespeare's Prince Hal!

For purposes of choice, any arbitrary strictly decreasing function of the prior probability $p(h)$ would suffice to indicate the degree of surprise, as a choice criterion (an 'ordinal utility', to use the economist's language). It is therefore not clear why considerable attention was paid, at least in early literature, to a particular numerical function that could or should be used as 'measure of information' – such as

$$1/p; \quad 1-p; \quad \log(1/p).$$

Now with regard to Question (B). Denote by $p(h \mid e)$ the posterior probability of the hypothesis h, given the evidence e. The proposed criterion is this: of the two hypotheses, h_1 and h_2, choose h_1 if

$$p(h_1 \mid e) > p(h_2 \mid e).$$

Remember that 'surprise' was the proposed criterion for choosing the hypothesis to be tested, while posterior probability is a criterion for choosing the hypothesis to be accepted. Naturally they may very well induce quite different orderings. Yet, perhaps because each of them seems to be a 'good thing', attempts were made, as we have mentioned already, to justify some particular increasing functions of both surprise and posterior probability

$$f(1-p(h), p(h \mid e)),$$

as a guide for the 'choice' between hypotheses, as if the Questions (A) and (B) described the same choice situation. In fact both the sum and the product of posterior probability and of some measure of surprise have been discussed.[2]

In the present paper, Questions (A) and (B) will be separated. As to (A): In Sections I through IV of the paper, we use some known results of information economics and statistical decision theory, valid for any 'benefit function' of actions and outside events. We exemplify these results on the simple case of a 'satisficing bettor' which will be later used as a first approximation to a 'scientist' as one who 'cares for truth only'. In general, the set of events that are benefit-relevant for the scientist can be interpreted as his 'problem'. Its subsets are 'hypotheses'. Then, these can be interpreted as ('noiseless') 'answers', or 'messages'. A partition of the problem into mutually exclusive and exhaustive hypotheses is, then, a 'question', or 'information system'. One can completely order the available information systems according to their 'values' (highest achievable expected benefits). The same complete ordering is induced by the systems' 'gains' (excess of the values over those achievable under ignorance). A different complete ordering obtains when allowing for the cost of each information system. To derive these orderings is called for by our Question (A1) above. (A1) must replace (A) since we cannot choose answers, only questions. Nevertheless, the value of an individual answer (later to be interpreted as one of the scientist's hypotheses) can be defined, as the maximal expected benefit obtained when this answer happens to be true. It is shown that this value of an answer and thus of a scientist's hypothesis, does not necessarily increase with the degree of surprise. Nor, in general, does the (meaningfully defined) 'gain' carried by the answer. However, in one case, the criterion of 'surprise' as desirable is vindicated: when the compared answers (hypotheses) are mutually exclusive and are 'perfect', in the sense of specifying precisely a unique component of the scientist's problem (i.e. an event that is, for him 'benefit-relevant'). In this case, the least surprising hypothesis carries indeed the smallest gain.

The above Questions (A2), on optimal tests, and (B), on the optimal rule of accepting a hypothesis, are handled in Section V. Under certain plausible assumptions, the criterion of maximizing posterior probability is vindicated, – but not in any combination with the 'degree of surprise'.

In Section VI, the 'pure truth-seeker' is postulated, then replaced by one for whom different problems (sets of benefit-relevant events) differ in *importance*. Other generalizations of the concept 'scientist' are also described, and the problem of multiple criteria is discussed.

The scientist's *costs*, discussed in Section VII, include the cost of testing hypotheses, and also that of remembering and communicating them. This brings in the entropy formula, used to measure, in 'bits', the minimum expected length of a message. Viewed this way, a hypothesis involving fewer parameters expresses more 'orderliness' and is sometimes said to be more 'beautiful'.

Colin Cherry [9] distinguished between the 'semantic' information of inductive logic, the 'selective information' of coding theory, and the 'pragmatic information' to a user. By applying results of statistical decision theory and information economics and regarding the scientist as a particular kind of user, this paper extends, in a sense, pragmatic theory so as to cover the other two.

I. AN EXAMPLE

Suppose it is relevant for you to know which of the following four kinds of weather we shall have over the next weekend: will it be dry? will it rain? snow? hail? For example, suppose that you own a hotel, and your decisions as to the kind and number of needed personnel will bring different benefits (your profits, in this case), depending on the weather thus specified. We suppose for simplicity that further characteristics of that weekend, meteorological or otherwise (the amount of precipitation, the strength of wind, the outcome of that week's political elections) will have no such effects. The four stated alternative kinds of weather constitute, then, the set Z of *benefit-relevant events*, denoted by $z(=z_1, z_2, z_3, z_4)$, the four column heads of our Table I:

z_1	z_2	z_3	z_4
hail	snow	rain	dry

Consider now the following three questions, also listed in that Table:

Question Y : will it be dry or not?
Question Y' : will it be dry, will it rain, or neither?
Question Y'': will it be dry, will it rain, will it snow, or will it hail?

Each *question* can be regarded as a set whose elements are *answers*: Harrah [13], Picard [38]. The answers are denoted in Table I by lower-case letters. For example, y'_1 ('it will snow or hail') is one possible answer to, and thus one element of, Y'.

The questions we consider here are all 'noiseless', in the sense that, given an event, only one answer will be forthcoming. A question that is 'noisy' (or 'stochastic') with respect to our four benefit-relevant kinds of future weather would be, for example: 'is to-day's barometric pressure high or low?'. If the weekend will be dry it is probable but not fully certain that to-day's pressure should be high: it is not fully excluded that it might be low.

TABLE I

		Set Z of events z				

z_1 z_2 z_3 z_4 $z^o = z_4$

Prior probabilities

π_1 π_2 π_3 π_4
0.01   0.02   0.18   0.80

Question Y answers y	$p(y)$		$p(z\mid y)$			$\begin{array}{c}\max_z p(z\mid y)\\ =v(y)\end{array}$	$\begin{array}{c}p(z^o\mid y)\\ =v^o(y)\end{array}$	$g(y)$
$y_1=(z_1,z_2,z_3)$	0.20	0.05	0.05	0.90	0	0.90	0	0.90
$y_2=(z_4)$	0.80	0	0	0	1	1	1	0
						$V(Y)$	$V(Y^o)$	$G(Y)$
						0.98	0.80	0.18

Question Y' answers y'	$p(y')$		$p(z\mid y')$			$v(y')$	$v^o(y'')$	$g(y')$
$y'_1=(z_1,z_2)$	0.02	0.50	0.50	0	0	0.50	0	0.50
$y'_2=(z_3)$	0.18	0	0	1	0	1	0	1
$y'_3=(z_4)$	0.80	0	0	0	1	1	1	0
						$V(Y')$	$V(Y^o)$	$G(Y')$
						0.99	0.80	0.19

Question Y'' answers y''	$p(y'')$		$p(z\mid y'')$			$v(y'')$	$v^o(y'')$	$g(y'')$
$y''_1=(z_1)$	0.01	1	0	0	0	1	0	1
$y''_2=(z_2)$	0.01	0	1	0	0	1	0	1
$y''_3=(z_3)$	0.18	0	0	1	0	1	0	1
$y''_4=(z_4)$	0.80	0	0	0	1	1	1	0

As indicated on Table I, every answer to a noiseless question is a subset of the set Z of benefit-relevant events. Thus, a noiseless question such as Y is a *partition* of the set Z as this term is usually defined, since

$$Y=(y_1,y_2); \qquad y_1=(z_1,z_2,z_3), \qquad y_2=(z_4);$$
$$Z=(z_1,z_2,z_3,z_4):$$

the elements of Y are subsets of Z, and every element of Z belongs to one and only one of these subsets. (Only noiseless questions are partitions of Z; noisy ones will appear in Section V, as 'evidence'.)

If question Y' could be answered as easily as question Y, e.g., without adding to or refining the weatherman's instruments and thus adding to the costs of his services, you would prefer to ask Y'. This is because if, having asked it, you receive either the answer y'_1 ('it will snow or hail') or the answer y'_2 ('it will rain'); then you know also the correct answer (*viz.*, y_1, 'it won't be dry') to question Y, while the remaining answer y'_3 to Y' ('it will be dry') is identical with the remaining answer y_2 to Y. Thus every answer to Y' implies some answer to Y. But the converse is not true. We can also say that each answer to Y' is *stronger* than some unique answer to Y. And we say that, of the two questions, Y' and Y, the former is the *finer* and the latter is the *coarser* of the two. In the trivial case of two identical sets we shall say that each is both finer and coarser than the other.

To be sure, not all questions about Z are thus pairwise comparable with respect to the relation 'coarser than'. For example, a question Y''' (not in the Table) defined as 'will it snow or won't it?' is neither coarser nor finer than Y: the answer 'it will snow' implies, and is not implied by, 'it won't be dry'; but the answer 'it won't snow' is implied by, and does not imply, 'it will be dry'.

The relation 'coarser than' induces thus only a partial ordering on the set of possible questions Y, Y', Y'', Y''',.... If two questions are not comparable with respect to this relation, and still can be answered at equal cost, the preference ranking will depend on who asks the questions, e.g. whether your hotel is a ski-resort in need of snow and also, as we shall see, on what probabilities you assign to the four benefit-relevant events.

If, more generally, different questions call for different costs of answering them, the ordering of preference between them will depend on the questioner (does he own a ski-resort and what event probabilities does he assume?), even when one question is definitely finer than the other. In brief, the *benefit* that can be achieved, on the average, from knowing the correct answer to a question must be weighed against the necessary *cost* of asking the question.

An alternative word for 'question' will catch some further properties of the underlying concept; the word is: 'information system'. An 'answer' is, in general, obtained by processing some evidence; and it will often have to be memorized and/or communicated, as in our example where the weatherman is not identical with the hotelier. Thus the answers are produced, in general, by a system (a chain, a network) of processors, before they are received and acted upon by the decision-maker. He responds to these *messages* by choosing an action among those available to him.

We shall use the terms 'question' and 'information system', 'answer' and 'message' interchangeably. In Section V, 'hypotheses' will be regarded as 'answers'.

The reader will have noticed that we are considering decision-making on two levels. Given the information system, decisions are made as to which action to take in response to each message. Neglecting, in effect, the 'cost of decision-making' (*not* the cost of information) we shall assume that the *best* action is taken. More precisely stated, so as to allow for the case when two or more actions are available that are not worse than any other available ones, we assume that one of these '*optimal actions*' is taken by the 'ideal actor'.

On another and, in a sense, 'higher' level, an *optimal information system* must be chosen; that is, one that is not worse than any other available information system. The maker of this higher level decision may be called the *meta-decider* (he is sometimes called 'organizer', as in Marschak and Radner [32]) thus distinguishing him from the *actor*. Of course, they may happen to be the same person.

The preference ordering between questions, not between answers, is a practical one, in that it does influence our choices. We subscribe to a newspaper precisely because we don't know the answer, only the questions that it will answer. Accordingly we shall be able to define, the 'value' and the 'gain' associated with a question, an information system. And if the cost required exceeds the gain, the system should not be implemented, built, bought, hired.

Later we shall discuss the preference between hypotheses (answers) as to which one should be accepted, given the evidence. This is different from the preference ordering of hypotheses that has been the subject of lively discussion in the literature on inductive logic and the scientific method: as if, in some sense, one answer would 'make you happier' than another. For example, it has been suggested that a strong hypothesis should be preferred to a weaker one. But, as remarked by Harrah [13] the message 'you will be robbed and murdered' is hardly preferable to the weaker one, 'you will be robbed'. However, it will be shown possible to discuss such problems after defining the 'value' and the 'gain' associated with an answer.

II. SOME CONCEPTS FORMALIZED

Consider a decision-maker who is consistent in the sense that he obeys certain postulates (such as the transitivity of preferences) which Frank Ramsey [43] regarded as transparent enough to call them an 'extension of logic'. Jointly, they are sufficient and necessary for the existence of the decision-maker's 'personal probabilities' of events and the 'personal utilities' of the consequences of his actions, given the event. The utilities are real numbers and the personal probabilities have the (measure-theoretical) properties of mathematical probabilities. To each action can thus be assigned the mathematical expectation of the utility of its consequences; and of any two actions, the consistent decision-maker will choose the one with higher expected utility. Contemporary logicians have paid attention to this approach: for example, Carnap [6, 7, 8], Hintikka [17].

For our purposes, what will be simplest to do, is, in effect, often what is done in practice; that is to conceive of utility as the difference between *benefit* and *cost*, so that both are measured in 'utility units'. These are arbitrary to the extent that the ordering of expected utilities by their magnitudes, and thus the preference ordering of actions, is obviously invariant under any increasing linear transformation (i.e., any change of units and of origin) of the utility amounts. Define:

benefit $b = \beta(a_k, z_i)$, where
a_k, an element of A, is a 'benefit-relevant action'
z_i, an element of Z, is a 'benefit-relevant event', and
β is the 'benefit-function', characteristic of the decision-maker.

For brevity, we shall often write $\beta(a, z)$, omitting the subscripts. For mathematical simplicity, but admitting that this excludes some important problems, we shall consider only the case when the sets Z and A are both finite, permitting us to write β occasionally as a matrix, $\beta = [\beta_{az}]$.

The function β depends on the ways in which, in the decision-maker's view, a given event and a given action result in a particular consequence, and also on his 'tastes' that assign utilities to consequences. Thus if z

has the values 'it will snow' and 'it won't', and a has the values 'take the skis with you' and 'leave them at home' the benefit function will be different for a ski enthusiast and for an old man longing for fresh mountain air and sun. In what will follow the 'tastes' of the scientist will indeed deserve our attention.

The personal (or, with Carnap [8], initial) probabilities are also characteristic of the decision-maker.[3] Write:

π_z = probability of the event z, $(z = z_1, ..., z_m)$, and sometimes, for brevity, $\pi_{z_i} = \pi_i$; and

π = probability vector $(\pi_1, ..., \pi_m)$, characterizing the initial probability distribution, the decision-maker's 'beliefs', as distinct from his 'tastes' that are reflected in the function β.

As in the previous section, we denote the 'answers', or 'messages received by the decision-maker' (*viz.*, the 'actor') or, briefly, 'messages', by

y,   , elements of the set Y,
y' , elements of the set Y', etc.

where, with Y, Y', ..., finite,

$$y = y_1, ..., y_n; \qquad y' = y'_1, ..., y'_{n'}; \text{ etc.}$$

We have called Y, Y', ... 'questions' or 'information systems' ('systems' for brevity). In our simple case, that of 'noiseless' systems, to each event z in Z corresponds some unique message y in Y, and, similarly, some unique message y' in Y', etc.

A *message* will be called *perfect* if it is associated with one event only; otherwise it is called imperfect. Perfect messages are, in our example, the messages y_2 in Y, and y'_3 in Y'. When all messages of a system are perfect – as is the case with system Y'' – the *system* is called *perfect*.

A few words may be added about more general *noisy* systems. These were treated elsewhere; Marschak and Miyasawa [31], Marschak [23, 26, 27], partly following the lead of Blackwell [1], and Blackwell and Girshick [2]. A system Y is characterized by the conditional probabilities ('likelihoods') of a message, given the event:

(II.1) $p(y \mid z)$, $y \in Y$, $z \in Z$.

When all $p(y \mid z)$ are 1 or 0, Y is noiseless.

Whether the system is noisy or not, a message y is a random occurence. In a noiseless system this is the case because y is a subset of the random set Z. (In the noisy case there is the additional uncertainty, given z, that a particular message y will be received.) Clearly the joint probability $p(y, z)$ that both y and z occur is, in the noiseless case

$$\text{(II.2)} \qquad p(y, z) = \begin{cases} \pi_z & \text{if} \quad z \in y \\ 0 & \text{if} \quad z \notin y \end{cases},$$

where $\in$, $\notin$ mean 'is in', 'is not in'. Now the 'marginal' probability, $p(y)$, that y occurs is defined as

$$p(y) = \sum_{z \in Z} p(y, z)$$
$$p(y) = \sum_{z \in y} p(y, z) + \sum_{z \notin y} p(y, z);$$

so that by (II.2)

$$\text{(II.3)} \qquad p(y) = \sum_{z \in y} \pi_z .$$

Further, the posterior probability of the event z, given the message y, is defined, for $p(y) \neq 0$, as

$$\text{(II.4)} \qquad p(z \mid y) = p(y, z)/p(y).$$

Hence by (II.2), (II.3)

$$\text{(II.5)} \qquad p(z \mid y) = \begin{cases} \pi_z / \sum_{z \in y} \pi_z & \text{if} \quad z \in y \\ 0 & \text{if} \quad z \notin y \end{cases}.$$

The marginal probabilities of messages and of the posterior probabilities of events, given a message, are entered on Table I accordingly.

It is seen that the probabilities $p(y, z)$, $p(y)$, $p(z \mid y)$ all depend: (1) on the initial probability distribution π, and (2) on the information system Y. Of these, π is given to, but Y is chosen by, the meta-decider.

III. VALUE OF SYSTEM AND OF MESSAGE;
GAIN FROM SYSTEM AND FROM MESSAGE

The value of a system Y, to be denoted by $V(y)$, will be defined as the expected benefit that is achieved if each message y is responded to by an optimal action. The expected benefit, B, is obtained by averaging the benefit, $\beta(a, z)$ over all possible events z and messages y:

(III.1)　　$B = \sum_y \sum_z p(y, z)\, \beta(a, z),$

where $\sum_y$, $\sum_z$ denote summation over all $y \in Y$, all $z \in Z$. Any function α that associates each message $y \in Y$ with some available action $a \in A$ is called *rule of action* (also 'decision function', 'strategy'). Thus $a = \alpha(y)$, and

(III.2)　　$B = \sum_y \sum_z p(y, z)\, \beta[\alpha(y), z] = B_{\pi\beta}(Y, \alpha);$

the last term on the right being written so as to emphasize that the expected benefit B depends on

(1) the initial probability function π and benefit function β, written as subscripts; they are *given* to the actor and the meta-decider;

(2) the *controlled* functions: α is chosen by the actor, Y by the meta-decider.

Write $\{\alpha\}$ for the set of all functions from the set Y of messages to the set A of available actions. To the 'ideal' actor (see Section I) all decision functions in $\{\alpha\}$ are available at no (or, more generally, at equal) 'cost of decision-making' – to be distinguished from the cost of information which is attached to Y. Denote by α^* an optimal decision function. Then the *value of the information system* is defined thus:

(III.3)　　$V(Y) = \max_{\alpha \in \{\alpha\}} B_{\pi\beta}(Y, \alpha) = B_{\pi\beta}(Y, \alpha^*) = V_{\pi\beta}(Y),$

with the two subscripts still indicating the givens, but with only one controlled variable, Y, left free, to be chosen by the meta-decider. More explicitly,

(III.4)　　$V(Y) = \max_{\alpha \in \{\alpha\}} \sum_y \sum_z p(y, z)\, \beta(\alpha(y), z) =$

　　　　　$= \sum_y \sum_z p(y, z)\, \beta(\alpha^*(y), z) \geq \sum_y \sum_z p(y, z)\, \beta(\alpha(y), z),\ \alpha \in \{\alpha\}.$

Now, the *conditionally expected benefit*, given a message y is

(III.5)　　$\sum_z p(z \mid y)\, \beta(a, z),$

a function of y and a. Denote its maximum value with respect to a at a fixed y, by

(III.6) $\quad v(y) = \max_{a \in A} \sum_z p(z \mid y)\,\beta(a, z) \geq$

$$\geq \sum_z p(z \mid y)\,\beta(a, z), \quad \text{all} \quad a \in A;$$

let a^y be that action a at which this maximum is achieved:

(III.7) $\quad v(y) = \sum_z p(z \mid y)\,\beta(a^y, z) \geq \sum_z p(z \mid y)\,\beta(a, z), \quad \text{all} \quad a \in A.$

Multiply by $p(y)$, a non-negative number, and add over all $y \in Y$. Then, since, by (II.4)

(III.8) $\quad p(y) \cdot p(z \mid y) = p(y, z),$

we have

(III.9) $\quad \sum_y p(y)\,v(y) = \sum_y \sum_z p(y, z)\,\beta(a^y, z) \geq$

$$\geq \sum_y \sum_z p(y, z)\,\beta(\alpha(y), z), \quad \text{all} \quad \alpha \in \{\alpha\}$$

having, in the last term on the right, used any arbitrary decision function α associating message y with action a. It follows from (III.4), (III.9) that

(III.10) $\quad a^y = \alpha^*(y)$

(III.11) $\quad \sum_y p(y)\,v(y) = V(Y).$

The quantity $v(y)$ is measured in utility units and may be called 'value of message', but only with some reservation, as already pointed out at the end of Section I. The meta-decider chooses the information system, computing the excess of its value (defined in (III.3)) over its cost. But he cannot make choices between messages. Or perhaps we can say that a message allowing the achievement of a higher conditionally expected benefit, is preferable, not in a sense of guiding one's choice but in the sense of 'making him happier'?

To illustrate, we shall use a particularly simple case of a 'bettor'. It will later help in the analysis of scientific decisions. Let the three information systems (questions) of Table I be considered by a man who can perform four actions, of which one and only one is appropriate to a given one of the four kinds of weather. Any matching of weather and action is equally good, any mismatching equally bad. There are thus only two levels of benefit, say r and s utility units, with $r > s$ (The man is thus a 'satisficer' in the sense of March and Simon [21], if system costs are neglected). By appropriately labelling the actions, so that action a_i matches event z_i, the benefit function is then

$$(\text{III.12}) \quad \beta(a_k, z_i) = \begin{cases} r & \text{as} \quad k = i \\ s & \text{as} \quad k \neq i \end{cases}; \quad r > s.$$

Our simple case is thus one of a man who bets on one of the possible events, receiving the amount r if he is right, and a smaller amount s if he is wrong.

If no other events and actions are under consideration, we can put $r = 1, s = 0$, since the results are not affected by the choice of unit and origin (linear transformation of measurements). We have then

$$(\text{III.13}) \quad \beta(a_k, z_i) = \delta_{ki} = \begin{cases} 1 & \text{as} \quad k = i \\ 0 & \text{as} \quad k \neq i \end{cases},$$

(δ_{ki} is called the 'Kronecker delta'). The conditionally expected benefit from an action a_k, given, for example, the answer y_1 to the question Y of Table I is, by (III.5),

$$(\text{III.14}) \quad \sum_{i=1}^{4} p(z_i \mid y_1) \beta(a_k, z_i) = \sum_{i=1}^{4} p(z_i \mid y_1) \delta_{ki} =$$

$$= p(z_k \mid y_1) \cdot 1 + \sum_{i \neq k} p(z_i \mid y_1) \cdot 0 = p(z_k \mid y_1).$$

Hence an optimal action a^{y_1} in response to message y_1 is an action that maximizes the posterior probability of the unknown event. It is best to bet on that event which, in the light of evidence, is the most probable, a posteriori! And the message value, that is, the maximal conditionally expected benefit, is

$$(\text{III.15}) \quad v(y_1) = \max_i p(z_i \mid y_1),$$

i.e., in this case, with the posterior probabilities computed using (II.5),

$$(\text{III.16}) \quad v(y_1) = \max\left(\frac{\pi_1}{\pi_1 + \pi_2 + \pi_3}, \frac{\pi_2}{\pi_1 + \pi_2 + \pi_3}, \frac{\pi_3}{\pi_1 + \pi_2 + \pi_3}, 0\right) =$$

$$= \max(0.05, 0.05, 0.18) = 0.18.$$

Generally, but still confining ourselves to our case of noiseless messages received by a 'satisficing bettor', i.e., assuming that every y in Y is a subset of Z, $y \subset Z$; and that the benefit $\beta(a, z) = \delta_{az}$, we obtain:

$$(III.17) \quad v(y) = (\max_{z \in y} \pi_z) / \sum_{z \in y} \pi_z$$

and since

$$(III.18) \quad p(y) = \sum_{z \in y} \pi_z,$$

$$(III.19) \quad V(Y) = \sum_{y \in Y} p(y) v(y) = \sum_{y \in Y} \max_{z \in y} \pi_z.$$

For example, $V(Y')$ in Table I could be computed both ways:

$$\sum_{y'} p(y') v(y') = (0.02)(0.50) + (0.18)(1) + (0.80)(1) = 0.99$$

$$\sum_{y'} \max_{z \in y'} \pi_z = 0.01 + 0.18 + 0.80 = 0.99.$$

We shall now propose definitions of the *gains* from messages and from systems; these are concepts that will prove useful for our analysis of some suggestions made in the literature on the logic of inductive science.

When actions must be taken in the absence of messages, on the basis of prior probabilities only (which, of course, need not be 'inborn' but may be posterior with respect to some previous evidence), we say that decisions are based on ignorance, or 'null-information', Y^o. The value of null-information is

$$(III.20) \quad V(Y^o) = \max_a \sum_z \pi_z \beta(a, z) = \sum_z \pi_z \beta(a^o, z),$$

so that a^o denotes an optimal action under ignorance. It is independent of any message. The difference

$$(III.21) \quad G(Y) = V(Y) - V(Y^o)$$

can be called the *gain from the information system* Y. Let $K(Y)$ be the cost of Y. The cost of null information is $= 0$. Hence the system Y can be chosen only if the *net gain* N is positive, that it is if

$$(III.22) \quad N(Y) = G(Y) - K(Y) > 0.^{4}$$

Given a message y, evaluate the maximum conditionally expected benefit that would be yielded by an action a^o that is optimal under ignorance. Call it

$$(III.23) \quad v^o(y) = \sum_z p(z \mid y) \, \beta(a^o, z).$$

The *gain from message* can be then defined as

$$(III.24) \quad g(y) = v(y) - v^o(y).$$

It is easily seen that

$$(III.25) \quad \sum_y p(y) \, v^o(y) = V(Y^o);$$

and by (III.11), (III.21), (III.24)

$$(III.26) \quad G(Y) = \sum_y p(y) \, g(y):$$

the system gain is the mean of message gains.

In our case of the 'satisficing bettor', $\beta(a_k, z_i) = \delta_{ki}$, we have

$$(III.27) \quad V(Y^o) = \max_i \pi_i = \pi^o, \quad \text{say};$$

and denoting by z^o the event with maximal prior probability π^o, (which for simplicity we shall assume unique)

$$(III.28) \quad v^o(y) = p(z^o \mid y),$$

$$(III.29) \quad g(y) = \max_i p(z_i \mid y) - p(z^o \mid y).$$

The gains $g(y)$ from messages and $G(Y)$ from systems are also computed in Table I.

IV. COARSENING A SYSTEM; WEAKENING A MESSAGE; SURPRISING MESSAGES

Given two information systems – call them Y and Y' – we say that Y' is more informative than Y' (in the sense of Blackwell [1]) if

$$(IV.1) \quad V_{\pi\beta}(Y') \geq V_{\pi\beta}(Y)$$

for all distributions π on Z and all benefit functions β on $A \times Z$. When Y, Y' are both noiseless we have the following theorem:

THEOREM *Y' is more informative than Y if and only if it is finer than Y.*

It will suffice to give the proof for the case of the 'satisfying bettor', with the value of an information system given in (III.19). Suppose Y, Y' are noiseless. Then every y in Y and every y' in Y' are subsets of Z, every z is in some y and also in some y'.

Suppose Y' is finer than Y (as is, for example, the case with the two systems thus denoted in Table I). The message y in Y is a union of some messages y' in Y'. Then

$$\text{(IV.2)} \qquad \max_{z \in y} \pi_z = \max_{y' \subset y} \max_{z \in y'} \pi_z \le \sum_{y' \subset y} \max_{z \in y'} \pi_z$$

for the expression on the left side of the inequality is only one (*viz.*, the maximal) component of the sum of non-negative numbers on the right side. Summing now both sides over all y in Y, by (III.19),

$$\text{(IV.3)} \qquad V(Y) = \sum_{y \in Y} \max_{z \in y} \pi_z \le \sum_{y \in Y} \sum_{y' \subset y} \max_{z \in y'} \pi_z =$$
$$= \sum_{y' \in Y} \max_{z \in y'} \pi_z = V(Y').$$

This result is valid for all probability distributions π. (It can be shown that it is also valid for all benefit functions β.)

On the other hand, suppose Y' is neither finer nor coarser than Y. For example, with $Z = (z_1, z_2, z_3, z_4)$, define

$$Y: y_1 = (z_1, z_2), \qquad y_2 = (z_3, z_4)$$
$$Y': y'_1 = (z_1, z_3), \qquad y'_2 = (z_2, z_4).$$

Let $\pi_1 > \max(\pi_2, \pi_3)$, and $\min(\pi_2, \pi_3) > \pi_4$. Then by (III.19)

$$V(Y) = \pi_1 + \pi_3 < V(Y') \quad \text{as} \quad \pi_2 > \pi_3$$
$$V(Y') = \pi_1 + \pi_2 < V(Y) \quad \text{as} \quad \pi_2 < \pi_3.$$

Thus, depending on the distribution π, the value of the system Y' is greater or less than the value of the system Y. (A similar reasoning would apply to cases when two messages from the two compared systems have more than one event in common, – thus completing the general proof.)[5]

The gain from an information system was defined in (III.21) as the excess of its value over the value (the maximum expected benefit) of null-information. It follows that

$G(Y') \geq G(Y)$ for all distributions π and all benefit functions β if and only if Y' is finer than Y.

These results conform with what we said in Section I. It was also mentioned there that the finer system is not necessarily the preferable one. The meta-decider will also pay attention to the difference (if any) in the system costs, comparing, in the notation of (III.22)

(IV.5) $N(Y') = G(Y') - K(Y')$ with $N(Y) = G(Y) - K(Y)$.

It will be recalled that a *system* Y' is said to be *finer* than Y (and Y coarser than Y') if to each message y' in Y' corresponds a unique weaker (possibly an identical) message y in Y. Is it then true to say that, somewhat analogous to the above theorems about system values V and system gains G, a *stronger* message always has a higher value v, or a higher gain g, than a weaker one?

The answer is: no. For suppose (without loss of generality, by properly labelling the events) that

(IV.6) $\begin{aligned} y &= (z_1, \ldots, z_h^*, \ldots, z_h) \\ y' &= (z_1, \ldots, z_h^*) \end{aligned}$

so that $h > h^*$ and y is weaker than y' (Compare, for example, on Table I, y_1 with y_1'; there $h = 3$, $h^* = 2$). Using (III.17), compare the respective denominators of the fractions that measure the values of the two messages:

(IV.7)   denominators: $\pi_1 + \cdots + \pi_h^* + \cdots + \pi_h > \pi_1 + \cdots + \pi_h^*$
numerators: $\max(\pi_1, \ldots, \pi_h^*, \ldots, \pi_h) \geq \max(\pi_1, \ldots, \pi_h^*)$

(for the larger set includes the maximal element of the smaller set, and possibly a still greater element: the tallest man in Africa cannot be taller than the tallest man in the world!). Thus the value of the weaker message has a larger denominator; but it may have a numerator sufficiently large to make the value of that message higher than that of the stronger massage. This is indeed the case in Table I, where

(IV.8) $v(y_1) = 0.90 > 0.50 = v(y_1')$.

Roughly: when I receive the weak message y_1 ('not dry') my best bet is on the event 'rain', with winning chance $=0.90$; but in response to the stronger message y'_1 ('either snow or hail') my winning chance is only $0.50!$ [6]

Table I also shows, given each message, the conditionally expected benefit v^o that would have been yielded if action a^o optimal under ignorance had been taken. This action was defined in (III.20), and v^o was defined in (III.23) and evaluated for the bettor's case in (III.28). The message gain, the difference $g = v - v^o$, is evaluated in (III.29). Note that under the assumed initial distribution π, the *a priori* most probable event, $z = z_4$, does not belong to the set $y_1 = (z_1, z_2, z_3)$ nor therefore to the smaller set $y'_1 = (z_1, z_2)$. As a result

$$(IV.9) \quad v^o(y_1) = v^o(y'_1) = 0$$

and by (IV.8)

$$(IV.10) \quad g(y_1) > g(y'_1).$$

To be sure this result was due to two conditions: (jointly sufficent and necessary, as can be shown) the numerators and denominators of the two expressions

$$v(y_1) = \frac{\max_{i \le h} \pi_i}{\sum_{i \le h} \pi_i} \quad \text{and} \quad v(y'_1) = \frac{\max_{i \le h*} \pi_i}{\sum_{i \le h*} \pi_i}; \quad h > h*$$

were such as to make $v(y_1)$ greater than $v(y'_1)$; and it was assumed that neither message included the (unique) maximally probable event, z^o:

$$z^o \notin y'_1 \quad \text{since} \quad z^o \notin y_1;$$

therefore $v^o(y'_1) = 0 = v^o(y_1)$.

We have assumed for simplicity that there is only one maximally probable event. It is then easily seen that, for any message y^*

$$(IV.11) \quad \text{if } z^o \begin{matrix} \in \\ \notin \end{matrix} y^* \quad \text{then} \quad v^o(y^*) = \begin{matrix} v(y^*) \\ 0 \end{matrix}, \quad g(y^*) = \begin{matrix} 0 \\ v(y^*) \end{matrix}$$

Suppose that, of two distinct messages which we shall call, for a moment, y and y', the latter is the stronger one. Applying (III.29) to (IV.11), we have:

$$\text{(IV.12)} \quad \begin{array}{l} \text{if} \quad z^o \in y' \quad \text{and therefore} \quad z^o \in y, \quad \text{then} \quad g(y')=g(y)=0 \\ \text{if} \quad z^o \notin y' \quad \text{but} \quad z^o \in y, \quad \text{then} \quad g(y')=v(y')>0, \; g(y)=0. \end{array}$$

Using the same distribution π as on Table I, we compare on Table II the values of, as well as the gains from, messages, of which some are stronger than other, and of which some do and some do not include the (unique) most probable event $z^o(=z_4)$. Table II has the same format as Table I except that the messages belong to overlapping information systems. The messages are denoted by $y^1, y^2, \ldots$. To begin with, Table II

TABLE II

	$p(y)$	π_1 0.01	π_2 0.01	π_3 0.18	π_4 0.80	$v(y)$	$v^o(y)$	$g(y)$
			$p(z\mid y)$					
$y^1=(z_1,z_2,z_3)$	0.20	1/20	1/20	9/10	0	9/10	0	9/10
$y^2=(z_1,z_3,z_4)$	0.99	1/99	0	18/99	80/99	80/99	80/99	0
$y^3=(z_1,z_2)$	0.02	1/2	1/2	0	0	1/2	0	1/2
$y^4=(z_1,z_3)$	0.19	1/19	0	18/19	0	18/19	0	18/19
$y^5=(z_3,z_4)$	0.98	0	0	18/19	80/98	80/98	80/98	0
$y^6=(z_3)$	0.18	0	0	1	0	1	0	1
$y^7=(z_4)$	0.80	0	0	0	1	1	1	0

illustrates again that the value of, and the gain from, a weaker message may or may not be less than those of a stronger one. This is brought out on Figure 1, an oriented graph in which the arrow $\rightarrow$ means 'weaker than', a relation that induces a partial ordering of messages. The pair of numbers attached to each y^i gives the value and the gain (in this order), given as decimal fractions to ease comparison. Our earlier counterexample against the preferability of the stronger of two messages is represented by the arrow on the extreme left (with y_1 and y'_1 of Table I now denoted, respectively, as y^1 and y^3).

Moreover, both Tables I and II illustrate the role of the relation 'more surprising than' discussed in the literature under various names such as 'having higher information content', or 'having higher information measure', these being some strictly decreasing functions of the marginal probability $p(y)$ of the message y, such as

$$1 - p(y); \quad 1/p(y); \quad \log(1/p(y)),$$

where the latter formula is apparently suggested by the 'bits' of the theory of communication (of which more latter, Section VII). All the above expressions induce the same complete ordering on the messages y, or on the events z if only perfect messages are considered.

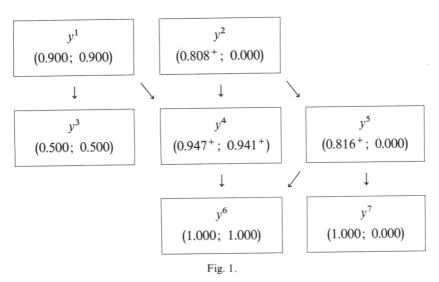

Fig. 1.

A strictly stronger message, being a proper subset of a weaker one, has a smaller probability and is therefore the more surprising of the two. Since, as we have shown, a stronger message may carry, for a 'satisficing bettor' both a smaller value and a smaller gain than a weaker one, he will not necessarily always prefer the stronger of two messages. To cover also other cases, in Table III we have arranged, the messages of Table II in an order ascending with the degree of surprise, for which the expression $1 - p(y)$ was chosen merely to fix the ideas. That the values and gains do not necessarily increase as surprise increases (i.e., $p(y)$ decreases), was also seen on Table I. These examples may, however, appear incomplete as they present as the less surprising, yet more valuable message, the stronger one only. For an example where none of the compared messages is stronger, and the less surprising is the preferable one,

TABLE III

	y^2	y^5	y^7	y^1	y^4	y^6	y^3
$1-p(y)$	0.01	0.02	0.20	0.80	0.81	0.82	0.98
$v(y)$	0.803^+	0.816^+	1.000	0.900	0.947^+	1.000	0.500
$g(y)$	0.000	0.000	0.000	0.900	0.947^+	1.000	0.500

a new set of events, $Z^* = (z_1^*, z_2^*, z_3^*, z_4^*, z_5^*)$ is entered on Table IV, where two mutually exclusive messages (belonging to the same information system) can be compared: y_2^* is less surprising than y_3^* yet carries higher value and gain. Underlying all these examples is, of course, the comparison of values defined in (III.17), (III.28).

TABLE IV

		π_1^* 0.60	π_2^* 0.20	π_3^* 0.10	π_4^* 0.05	π_5^* 0.05			
	$p(y^*)$			$p(z^* \mid y^*)$			$v(y^*)$	$v^o(y^*)$	$g(y^*)$
$y_1^* = (z_1^*)$	0.60	1	0	0	0	0	1	1	0
$y_2^* = (z_2^*, z_3^*)$	0.30	0	2/3	1/3	0	0	2/3	0	2/3
$y_3^* = (z_4^*, z_5^*)$	0.10	0	0	0	1/2	1/2	1/2	0	1/2

Particular attention should be given to the perfect messages, $y = (z_i)$ such as y_2, y_2', y_3', and $y_j = (z_j)$ $(j = 1, ..., 4)$ of Table I. Their value is always equal to 1 and thus exceeds the value $(\max_z p(z \mid y) < 1)$ of all imperfect ones. But, still confining ourselves to the case when there is only one maximally probable event, z^o, the gain from the perfect message $y = (z^o)$ is $1 - 1 = 0$ and is thus equal, by (IV.12), to the gain from any imperfect message that includes z^o among its elements (e.g., the messages y^2, y^5 of Table II); and is thus smaller than the gain from all imperfect messages that do not contain z^o. All other perfect messages carry the gain $1 - 0 = 1$. To summarize: denoting by y any imperfect message (a several-elements subset of Z) and by (z) a perfect message (a single-element subset of Z) we have, regarding their *values*:

(IV.13) $0 < v(y) < v((z)) = 1$;

and, denoting by y^o any imperfect message containing z^o among its elements, by $\bar{y}^o$ any other imperfect message and by $(\bar{z}^o)$ any other perfect message other than (z^o), we have, regarding the *gains* from these messages:

$$(\text{IV}.14) \quad 0 = g((z^o)) = g(y^o) < g(\bar{y}^o) < g((\bar{z}^o)) = 1.$$

Thus the suggestion that surprising messages are the more desirable ones is vindicated in the following form: the least surprising perfect message (*viz.*, (z^o)) carries the smallest gain, while all the other perfect messages carry the largest gain.[7]

V. THE SCIENTIST: PROBLEM, HYPOTHESES, EVIDENCE

The set Z of events z_i $(i = 1, ..., m)$, relevant to the scientist's benefit may be called his *problem*. A partition Y of Z, which we have called a 'question' Y, consisting of answers y, should be interpreted in the scientist's case, as a set, – now to be denoted by H, – whose elements are hypotheses, h. The reader will have no difficulty in replacing, in all expressions of the previous sections, Y, y by H, h.

To use Popper's example mentioned in the Introduction, the problem Z may consist in knowing the shape of a planet's orbit. Let $z_1 = $ 'it is a circle', $z_2 = $ 'it is an ellipse with unequal axes', $z_3 = $ 'it is neither'. Among the possible partitions of Z we have:

$$\begin{aligned}
&H^1 = (h_1^1, h_2^1); \; h_1^1 = (z_1), \; h_2^1 = (z_2, z_3): && \text{is it a circle or not?} \\
&H^2 = (h_1^2, h_2^2); \; h_1^2 = (z_1, z_2), \; h_2^2 = (z_3): && \text{is it an ellipse (with axes} \\
&(\text{V}.1) && \text{possibly equal) or not?} \\
&H^3 = (h_1^3, h_2^3, h_3^3); \; h_k^3 = (z_k), \; k = 1, 2, 3: && \text{which of the three listed} \\
& && \text{shapes is the true one?}
\end{aligned}$$

Given the problem $Z = (z_1, ..., z_m)$, the scientist's benefit-relevant actions are (or at least include) these: to assert that a particular z_k $(k = 1, ..., m)$ is true. This is not the same thing as to accept a hypothesis h, a subset of Z, – except when h happens to be 'perfect', i.e., to be a single-element subset. For example, to accept the two-elements hypothesis h_2^1 in (V.1), that the orbit is not a circle, still leaves the scientist uncertain whether it is an ellipse or not. And this is relevant, given his problem Z. Having accepted some hypothesis h, he can only revise the probabilities assigned to the elements z of the problem: instead of the initial probabilities π_z he has now (cf. (II.5))

(V.2) $p(z \mid h) = \begin{cases} \pi_z / \sum\limits_{z \in h} \pi_z & \text{if} \quad z \in h \\ 0 & \text{if} \quad z \notin h \end{cases}.$

We can say that, after having accepted a hypothesis, the scientist still has to decide further on which element z of his problem he has to 'bet'. He may also have other decisions at his disposal such as to do further research. We do not yet specify his benefit function, $\beta(a, z)$. In particular, we don't have to assume that he is a 'satisficing bettor' in the sense of our Section III, – although this is an interesting special assumption.

Hypotheses are accepted on the basis of *evidence*. Evidence is a random occurence. Inconveniently, the word has no plural, yet we must distinguish between the particular evidence observed, to be denoted by e, an 'observation', and the test (experiment) E, i.e., the set of possible observations e. In general, and unlike the set H, the set E is *not* a partition of Z. Rather, it is noisy, and is characterized by the conditional probability $p(e \mid h, z)$ that e is observed, given h and z. This determines the joint distribution

(V.3) $p(e, h, z) = p(h, z) \cdot p(e \mid h, z).$

Having chosen the question H and having chosen and performed the experiment E, two decisions must be made: (1) given the observation e, which hypothesis h to accept? and (2) given the accepted hypothesis h, which action a to take? The scientist's action a may consist in asserting that a particular element z of the problem Z is true; but other actions may be also available to him, – see Section VI, about 'suspending judgement' and the planning of further research.

The following two conditions will be shown to be jointly sufficient for the proposal of accepting a hypothesis h with maximal posterior probability $p(h \mid e)$, in a sense somewhat modifying that suggested by philosophers of science.

Condition 1. The probability of an observation e depends on h but not on z:

(V.4) $p(e \mid h, z) = p(e \mid h).$

That is, the evidence, given the hypothesis, is equally probable for all the benefit-relevant events of which the hypothesis is a set.

Condition 2. For any given benefit function β of action and event, the benefit function $\beta*$ of accepted hypothesis, action and event is

$$(V.5) \quad \beta*(h, a, z) = \begin{cases} \beta(a, z) & \text{if } z \in h \\ 0 & \text{if } z \notin h \end{cases}.$$

(Note that this condition fixes the zero-point of the utility scale!) Remembering that h depends on e, we can write the *expected benefit* of the pair (E, H) thus:

$$(V.6) \quad B(E, H) = \sum_e \sum_z p(e, h, z) \, \beta*(h, a, z),$$

where the summation is over the sets E, Z. Then our two conditions imply

$$(V.7) \quad B(E, H) = \sum_e \sum_{z \in h} p(h, z) \, p(e \mid h) \, \beta(a, z);$$

and since by definition

$$(V.8) \quad p(h, z) = p(z \mid h) \, p(h); \quad \text{and} \quad p(e \mid h) = p(e) \, p(h \mid e)/p(h),$$

$$(V.9) \quad B(E, H) = \sum_e p(e) \, p(h \mid e) \sum_{z \in h} p(z \mid h) \, \beta(a, z).$$

Note that the sum on the extreme right, the conditionally expected benefit, given the hypothesis (cf. (III.5)), is by (V.2) equal to

$$(V.10) \quad \sum_{z \in h} \beta(a, z) \, \pi_z / \sum_{z \in h} \pi_z.$$

Now, h (for given e) and a (for given h) should be chosen so as to maximise $B(E, H)$, to yield the *value* of the pair (E, H):

$$(V.11) \quad V(E, H) = \sum_e p(e) \max_h [p(h \mid e) \max_a \sum_{z \in h} p(z \mid h) \, \beta(a, z)].$$

Thus the hypothesis accepted must have maximal posterior probability, weighed by the expected benefit from the action that is optimal in response to that hypothesis.

As to the choice of the optimal pair (E, H), the costs associated with it must be deducted. These are the costs of testing and the costs of remembering and communicating. Both are, in general, random quantities since they may depend on which hypothesis happens to be true. For example the size, and hence the cost, of a sequential sample depends on the properties of the studied population. And an accepted hypothesis may be more or less difficult to remember and communicate, depending on its 'simplicity' – see Section VII. Denoting by $k(E, h)$, the cost of applying a test E when the true hypothesis is h, we obtain, as the expected cost of a question H,

$$(V.12) \quad K(E, H) = \sum_{h \in H} p(h) \, k(E, h),$$

where $p(h) = \sum_{z \in h} \pi_z$. And the pair (E, H) will be preferred to (E', H') if

$$(V.13) \quad V(E, H) - K(E, H) > V(E', H') - K(E', H').$$

VI. IS THE SCIENTIST A 'PURE TRUTH-SEEKER'?

One who 'cares for truth only' or, in other words, is a 'pure truthseeker' can be defined by a benefit function of the form

$$(VI.1) \quad \beta(a_k, z_i) = \delta_{ik}$$

as in (III.13): a 'satisficing bettor'. Then, under Conditions 1 and 2 of the previous section, the conditionally expected benefit, given the hypothesis, i.e., the expression (V.10), becomes equal to 1, so that by (V.11)

$$(VI.2) \quad V(E, H) = \sum_{e} p(e) \max_{h} p(h \mid e):$$

the pure truth-seeker choses the hypothesis with maximal posterior probability and has no other decisions to make.

When all hypotheses h in H are perfect in the sense of being single-element subsets of the problem Z, the pure truth-seeker we have defined coincides with the scientist discussed by various philosophers recently: for example, by Levi [19], Kyburg [18], Hilpinen [16]. Thus, z_i in (VI.1) is replaced by $h = (z_i)$: and the benefit is the 'epistemic utility' which Hempel [15] had suggested to assign to the assertions of a true and of a false hypothesis. However, impotant generalizations of the 'scientist' model, partly proposed by the same philosophers, can be discussed more fully when other partitions H of the problem Z are admitted, besides the 'perfect' one. We have just seen that for the desired result (VI.2), that restriction (which is clearly stronger than the Conditions 1 and 2) is not necessary.

One can generalize the 'pure truth-seeker' assumption (VI.1) in various directions (besides its extension to infinite sets). I do think it would still be fruitful to apply in each such generalized case the same optimization principles as those stated here previously.

To begin with one generalization, not every problem is equally 'important', either to a scientist or to a judge of his project, each problem being defined as a set of some 'events': such as the set of states of future weather, or the set of values of some physical or psychological parameter, or perhaps the set of various possible probability distributions of some variables.[8] One simple way to take this into account is to replace (VI.1) by the more general

$$(VI.3) \qquad \beta(a_k, z_i) = \delta_{ik} r(Z),$$

where the (positive) number $r(Z)$ measures the *importance* of the problem Z.

This increasing linear transformation does not affect the ranking of the values $V(E, H)$ for a fixed problem Z. But the ranking of the *net* values (in excess of costs) is affected. And of course the ranking of pairs (H, Z) and of the triples (E, H, Z) becomes possible, guiding those who ask: is it worthwhile to pursue this rather than that other line of research?

This generalization, still assigning for a given problem equal utility to all true assertions and another equal utility to all false ones, is no doubt too special. A somewhat greater variety of payoffs is implied in a suggestion made by Hintikka [17], that gain from a true assertion should be equal to the loss from its denial. (Note that this fixes a zero-point on the utility scale!).

It has been suggested by Menges [35], that if z_i is in some sense close to z_j then, for any action a, $|\beta(a, z_i) - \beta(a, z_j)|$ should be small. This is a very realistic idea, especially if the z are real numbers. One might add a similar requirement for the case of any two actions, a_g, a_h close to each other, so that, for all z, the difference $|\beta(a_g, z) - \beta(a_h, z)|$ be small; or further, require β to be a concave function, such as that popular criterion, the squared error of an estimate a of the parameter z: $-(a-z)^2$.

Instead of making an assertion the scientist may suspend judgement. While maintaining that all other actions of the scientist yield utility 1 if they are true statements and 0 if they are false, Hilpinen [16], proposes that suspension of judgement yields, for all z, the utility u (say), with $0.5 \leq u \leq 1$.

Allowing for suspension of judgement is an extremely important idea. It opens up the field of scientific planning over time. As was hinted in the first paragraph of this paper, any theory of information and decision must deal with time sequences of actions and of events. With the two independent variables of the benefit function thus interpreted, the set of action variables should, furthermore, include collecting and utilizing new evidence. Stated more precisely for the case of the scientist: suspending judgement is not a single action but a set. He may repeat the same test E or perform a different one on the same set H of hypotheses. Such is sequential sampling, a special case of 'dynamic programming' (see, e.g., Chernoff and Ray [10]; also Marschak [22], Miyasawa [37]). But the scientist may also decide to shift to a different partition, H', of the same problem Z. Finally, he can change the problem itself! A problem, or its partition into hypotheses, may gradually cease to be fruitful – following somewhat the observed S-shaped curve of technological developments of a given principle: speeding-up, then slowing-down (see, e.g., Th. Marschak et al. [33]). A person of genius may foresee this farther into the future than one with mere talent.

Admittedly, then, detailed scientific planning over wide time horizons is difficult or unfeasible, – or, what is the same thing, its cost is prohibitive –, given the psychology of men and the physics of computers: just as it is costly or unfeasible to evaluate the number π to very many digits. Mathematics and logic, including decision logic, are not the same thing as psychology. The growth of science through the change of hypotheses and problems, an awe-inspiring subject that has attracted men of the stature of Polanyi [39], and Popper, must remain a reasonable mixture of logic and psychology[9]; and even of sociology, to account for interaction among scientists, and between them and the rest of society.

The search for a proper balance between pure logic and the psychology and sociology of the feasible has also led to questioning the applicability of a single numerical criterion (the expected utility) as a guide to the scientist. Michalos [36], considers the expected utility approach ineffective, for "it requires a more sophisticated sort of information than is now or will be in the foreseeable future available". He lists several benefit criteria ("simplicity, explanatory power, precision of predictions, coherence with theories in other domains,...") and several cost criteria ("set-up time, computational effort, special facilities, technical assistance, money operationalization, etc."). Competing theories (before as well as after testing, I presume) are characterized by ranks attached, for each, to each criterion. This suffices for deciding between two theories – provided, of course that the vector formed by those rank numbers for one theory dominates the corresponding vector of another. As usual, an ordering of vectors is only a partial one. It is not clear what the scientist should decide, when one theory does better on one criterion, but worse on another, than its rival.

However, it is not really necessary to assign any numbers, not even rank numbers, to any individual criterion. It is enough to assign a number to each result of action, given the event, without representing each result as a bundle of critieria; although such representation (as in beauty contests and in the evaluation of chess positions by computers) does help in practice, – diminishing, in fact, the cost of decision-making. True, the expected utility approach requires the number assigned to each result of action and event to be on an 'interval scale' (i.e., fixed except for the choice of unit and origin), not a mere ranking. There is considerable literature on the needed soul-searching by the decision-maker, and some experience of cost-benefit analysis done by public agencies and in private business.

Sometimes utility is assumed to be additively separable into numerical criteria (e.g., Fishburn [12], Raiffa [42]). In the present paper, I have not gone that far, but have still assumed utility to be additively separable into overall benefit and overall cost. The reason for this is itself a decision criterion: "... pedagogical simplicity, ..., ... teachability", in the words of Bar-Hillel [5], another strong proponent of the multi-criterion approach.[10]

VII. COSTS. BITS AND BEAUTY

"What about the case when a severe testing of the highest-ranking theory will cost a few million dollars, whereas the next-highest-ranking theory can be tested for a few thousand dollars only? Is it a debasement of the lofty ideals of scientific methodology to bring in cost and monetary considerations?..." – As an economist I am much encouraged by these words of Bar-Hillel the philosopher, [5].

The cost $K(E, H)$ in (V.12) includes, besides cost of testing, also the cost of remembering and communicating. This is of some special interest as it is, I think, related to the 'teachability' and 'simplicity' just mentioned, – sometimes called the 'beauty' of a theory. Consider these two questions:

1.   Under which of two specified locations, equally deep below, is there oil?

2.   On which of the 64 fields of a chessboard covered with a light blanket is there a tablet of aspirin?

Assuming equal and non-null probabilities in both cases (i.e., $\frac{1}{2}$ and $\frac{1}{64}$, respectively) for each potential oil location and each chessboard field, the number of bits is: $\log_2 2 = 1$ in the case of oil, $\log_2 64 = 6$ in the case of aspirin. Clearly these numbers have no relation to the cost of the necessary inquiry which is very large in the case of oil and very small (just to remove the blanket!) in the case of aspirin. Nor is the number of bits related to the value that the user will receive after the hypotheses are tested: millions from the oil find, a relief of a trivial headache from the aspirin tablet!

What is related to the count of bits is the cost of remembering and communicating. In a binary code, just one digit is needed to identify in an unambigous, 'uniquely decodable' manner, the true location of oil, six digits to identify the chessboard field with that tablet. Correspondingly, a larger memory device is needed in the latter case. Further: if, to communicate the accepted hypothesis a single telegraph wire is used in both cases, there will be a difference in the time needed. Or, to achieve equal time, a six-wires cable (a 'channel with higher capacity') will have to be used to communicate the location of the aspirin tablet. Both wires and time are costly.

Werner Heisenberg reports [14], that Einstein talked to him, some 50 years ago, about Mach's call for 'simplicity' of theories on grounds of 'economy of thought'. To Einstein, this was 'suspiciously commercial'. It seems, he preferred to see in simplicity, or orderliness, a property of nature itself, – assigning to it, we would say now, a high initial probability. But what is simplicity of theory? It is also called beauty, and it is worth remembering Kant's pronouncement, in the *Kritik der Urteilskraft*, that a circle is beautiful because to describe it just two things need to be stated: the position of the center and the length of the radius. Just few digits, we would now say, to communicate or memorize![11] Is it a debasement (to repeat those words of Bar-Hillel) to talk here of economy?

University of California, Los Angeles, U.S.A.

NOTES

* Acknowledgements are due to the Alexander von Humboldt Foundation, to the Institute of Economic and Social Sciences, University of Bonn, and to the U.S. Office of Naval Research.
[1] Henceforth, the same symbol $p(.)$ will indicate any probability function, without risking ambiguity: for the domain of the function is indicated by the symbols within the parentheses.
[2] See, for example Hintikka [17] and an account of some of Popper's and Carnap's proposals, by Bar-Hillel [5].
[3] On the 'intersubjective' nature of observed frequencies as approximations to personal probabilities, see Marschak [25, 30]. In another paper [24] this author tried to present, using not very rigorous mathematics, the original results of Ramsey [43], DeFinetti [11], and Savage [44], and also discussed the relation of such 'logic of decision-making' to its 'psychology', as presented by Luce and Suppes [20].
[4] In Marschak and Radner [32], $G(Y)$ was called information value, but the present terminology seems preferable.
[5] Instead of fixing β and varying π, we might have fixed π and varied β as in Marschak and Radner [32].
[6] In Section I, we mentioned Harrah's preference for the weak message 'you will be robbed' as against the stronger one, 'you will be robbed and murdered'. This involves a benefit matrix other than that of our bettor. The reader may construct such a matrix, with three events – 'robbed and murdered', 'robbed and not murdered' and 'neither' – and three actions such as 'safeguard your valuables and make last will', 'safeguard them, but no last will', 'do nothing'. He will find that the stronger message may be worse than the weaker one, but that the finer system is not worse than the coarser one.
[7] This result was elaborated in Marschak [29], where the case of noisy messages was also treated – but always comparing mutually exclusive messages only.
[8] The latter case is essentially the description of the 'theoretical scientist', whom Carnap contrasts in one of his latest writings [8], with the 'practical man', a utility maximizer: the theoretical scientist should describe his "knowledge... by a specification of a probability distribution". But this is precisely the way in which 'Bayesian statistics' is usually presented: the unknown 'state' (our event z) is a point in the space of probability distributions. Using the benefit function (VI.1), the theoretical scientist can, then, still be regarded as a 'practical man'.

Actually, the 'practical man' of Carnap's example is an engineer just sophisticated enough to understand the theoretician's (a meteorologist's) prediction of an interval of temperatures but not of their whole probability distribution. It seems that this brings in the criterion (and the cost of) 'teachability' to be dealt with in the next Section. Not all codes are available, either on the sending or, as here, on the receiving side. This may call for redundancy or, as in this case, for a coarsening.

[9] "Human thought is better characterized by something like Molly Bloom's soliloquy then by, say, a proof in symbolic logic", (Quillian [41]).

[10] Like Carnap [8], and others, Bar-Hillel was particularly concerned with the coexistence of 'surprise' and posterior probability as two criteria. We have shown above that the worry is without foundation: posterior probability $p(h \mid e)$ guides the acceptance of hypothesis, the 'surprise' (measured, for example by $1 - \sum_{z \in h} \pi_z$) was supposed to (but hardly can) guide the choice of the hypothesis to be tested.

[11] In coding theory, the entropy formula is derived by minimizing the expected number of digits per message, subject to a decodability constraint (called the Kraft inequality). It is therefore indeed a measure of disorder in the sense just stated. It is also so described occasionally by physicists although they seem to derive it without minimizing anything: as the logarithm of the approximate probability of a given frequency distribution (of energy levels among particles, for example). See Schroedinger [46].

BIBLIOGRAPHY

[1] Blackwell, D., 'Equivalent Comparisons of Experiments', *Annals of Mathematical Statistics* **24** (1953).
[2] Blackwell, D. and Girshick, A., *Theory of Games and Statistical Decisions*, Wiley, 1954.
[3] Bar-Hilllel, Y. and Carnap, R., 'An Outline of a Theory of Semantic Information', Technical Report No. 247 of the *Research Laboratory for Electronics*, MIT, 1952. Reproduced as Chapter 15 of Y. Bar-Hillel, *Language and Information*, Addison-Wesley, 1964. See also Chapters 16 and 17.
[4] Bar-Hillel, Y., 'Essence and Significance of Information Theory'; in German: *Information über Informationen* (ed. by H. v. Ditfurth and W. D. Bach), Hoffmann und Campe, Hamburg, 1960.
[5] Bar-Hillel, Y., 'Poppers's Theory of Corroboration', *The Philosophy of Karl Popper* (ed. by P. A. Schilpp), The Free Press, 1973.
[6] Carnap, R., *Logical Foundations of Probability*, 2nd ed. (esp. Preface, p. XV), Chicago University Press, 1962.
[7] Carnap, R., 'The Aim of Inductive Logic', *Logic, Methodology and Philosophy of Science* (ed. by E. Nagel), Stanford University Press, 1962.
[8] Carnap, R., 'Probability and Content Measure', *Mind, Matter and Method* (in Honor of H. Feigl), University of Minneapolis Press, 1964.
[9] Cherry, Colin, *On Human Communication*, Wiley, 1957.
[10] Chernoff, H. and Ray, S. N., 'Bayes Sequential Sampling Inspection Plans', *Annals of Mathematical Statistics*, 1965.
[11] DeFinetti, B., 'Foresight, Its Logical Laws, Its Subjective Sources' (revised from French edition of 1937), *Studies in Subjective Probabilities* (ed. by H. Kyburg, and H. Smokler), New York 1964.
[12] Fishburn, P. C., *Utility Theory for Decision Making*, New York 1970.
[13] Harrah, D., *Communications: a Logical Model*, MIT Press, 1963.

[14] Heisenberg, W., *Der Teil und das Ganze*, Deutscher Taschenbuch Verlag, Munich, 1973.

[15] Hempel, C. G., 'Inductive Inconsistencies', *Synthese* **11** (1960).

[16] Hilpinen, R., 'Decision-Theoretic Approaches to Rules of Acceptance', *Contemporary Philosophy in Scandinavia* (ed. by R. Olson and A. Paul), Johns Hopkins Press, 1972.

[17] Hintikka, H., 'On Semantic Information', *Information and Inference* (ed. by H. Hintikka and P. Suppes), D. Reidel, Dordrecht, 1970.

[18] Kyburg, H., 'The Rule of Detachment in Inductive Logic', *Problems of Inductive Logic* (ed. by I. Lakatos), North-Holland, 1960.

[19] Levi, I., *Gambling with Truth*, A. Knopf, New York, 1967.

[20] Luce, R. D. and Suppes, P., 'Preference Utility and Subjective Probability', *Handbook of Mathematical Psychology* (ed. by R. D. Luce *et al.*), Vol. III, New York 1965.

[21] March, J. and Simon, H., *Organizations*, New York 1958.

[22] Marschak, J., 'Adaptive Programming', *Management Science* **9** (1963).

[23] Marschak, J., 'Economics of Inquiring, Communicating, Deciding', *Amer. Econ. Review* **68** (1968).

[24] Marschak, J., 'Decision-Making: Economic Aspects', *International Encyclopedia of Social Sciences*, Macmillan, 1968.

[25] Marschak, J., 'The Economic Man's Logic', *Induction, Growth, and Trade* (in honor of Sir Roy Harrod, ed. by M. Scott and W. Ellis), Oxford, Clarendon Press, 1970.

[26] Marschak, J., 'Economics of Information Systems', *Frontiers of Quantitative Economics* (ed. by M. Intriligator), North-Holland, 1971.

[27] Marschak, J., 'Optimal Systems for Information and Decision', *Techniques of Optization* (ed. by A. Balakrishnan), Academic Press, 1972.

[28] Marschak, J., 'Limited Role of Entropy in Information Economics', *Proceedings of the 5th Conference on Optimization Techniques* (International Federation for Information Processing), Rome 1973, Springer Verlag, Heidelberg/New York, forthcoming.

[29] Marschak, J., 'Prior and Posterior Probabilities', *Information, Inference and Decision* (ed. by G. Menges), D. Reidel, Dordrecht, 1974.

[30] Marschak, J., 'Intersubjektive Wahrscheinlichkeit', *Heidelberger Jahrbücher*, 1973.

[31] Marschak, J. and Miyasawa, K., 'Economic Comparability of Information Systems', *International Economic Review*, 1968.

[32] Marschak, J. and Radner, R., *Economic Theory of Teams*, Yale University Press, 1972.

[33] Marschak, Thomas, Glennan, Th. K., and Summers, R., *Strategy for Research and Development*, Springer, 1967.

[34] Menges, G., 'Semantische Information und Statistische Inferenz', *Biometrische Zeitschrift* **14** (1972).

[35] Menges, G., Personal communication, 1973.

[36] Michalos, A. C., 'Cost-Benefit versus Expected Utility Acceptance Rules', *Theory and Decision* **1** (1970) 61.

[37] Miyasawa, K., 'Information Structures in Stochastic Programming Problems', *Management Science* **14** (1968).

[38] Picard, C. F., 'Dépendance et Indépendance d'Expériences', *Comptes Rendus Acad. Sci. Paris* **276** (1973) Serie A.

[39] Polanyi, M., 'The Growth of Science in Society', *Criteria for Scientific Development: Public Policy and National Goals* (ed. by E. Shils), London 1968.

[40] Popper, K. R., *The Logic of Scientific Discovery*, Basic Books, New York, 1959 (Original edition in German, Vienna 1934).

[41] Quillian, M. R., Review of M. Cunningham's Intelligence, *Science* **178** (1972).

[42] Raiffa, H., *Decision Analysis*, Addison-Wesley, 1968.

[43] Ramsey, F. P., *Foundations of Mathematics and Other Logical Essays* (ed. by R. B. Braithwaite), New York 1957. See in particular the essays 'Truth and Probability' and 'Further Considerations', originally published in 1926 and 1928, respectively.

[44] Savage, L. J., *The Foundations of Statistics*, Dover Publications, New York, 1972 (original publication 1954).

[45] Savage, L. J., 'Elicitation of Personal Probabilities and Expectations', *Journ. Amer. Statistical Ass.* **66** (1971).

[46] Schroedinger, E., *Statistical Thermodynamics*, Cambridge University Press, 1948.

THEORY AND DECISION LIBRARY

An International Series in the Philosophy and Methodology
of the Social and Behavioral·Sciences

Editors:

GERALD EBERLEIN, *Universität des Saarlandes*
WERNER LEINFELLNER, *University of Nebraska*